The
National Express
Handbook

British Bus Publishing

Body codes used in the Bus Handbook series:

Type:

A   Articulated vehicle
B   Bus, either single-deck or double-deck
BC   Express - high-back seating in a bus body
C   Coach
M   Minibus with design capacity of 16 seats or less
N   Low-floor bus (*Niederflur*), either single-deck or double-deck
O   Open-top bus (CO = convertible - PO = Partial open-top)

Seating capacity is then shown. For double-decks the upper deck quantity is followed by the lower deck.

Door position:

C   Centre entrance/exit
D   Dual doorway.
F   Front entrance/exit
R   Rear entrance/exit (no distinction between doored and open)
T   Three or more access points

Equipment:

L	Lift for wheelchair	TV	Training Vehicle.
M	Mail compartment	RV	Used as tow bus or Engineers vehicle.
T	Toilet	w	Vehicle is withdrawn from service.

e.g. - B32/28F is a double-deck bus with thirty-two seats upstairs, twenty-eight down and a front entrance/exit.
N43D is a low-floor bus with two doorways.

Re-registrations:

Where a vehicle has gained new index marks the details are listed at the end of each fleet showing the current mark, followed in sequence by those previously carried starting with the original mark.

Other books in the series:

The Scottish Bus Handbook
The Ireland & Islands Bus Handbook
The North East Bus Handbook
The Yorkshire Bus Handbook
The Lancashire, Cumbria and Manchester Bus Handbook
The Merseyside and Cheshire Bus Handbook
The North and West Midlands Bus Handbook
The East Midlands Bus Handbook
The Welsh Bus Handbook
The South East Bus Handbook
The South West Bus Handbook

Annual books are produced for the major groups:

The Stagecoach Bus Handbook
The FirstBus Bus Handbook
The Arriva Bus Handbook
The National Express Handbook

Associated series:

The Hong Kong Bus Handbook
The Leyland Lynx Handbook
The Model Bus Handbook
The Postbus Handbook
The Overall Advert Book Volume 1
The Toy & Model Bus Handbook - Volume 1 - Early Diecasts

The Fire Brigade Handbook (fleet list of each local authority fire brigade)
The Police Range Rover Handbook

Some earlier editions of these books are still available. Please contact the publisher.

Contents

The National Express Handbook

The National Express Handbook is part of The Bus Handbook series that details the fleets of selected bus and coach operators. These Bus Handbooks are published by *British Bus Publishing* . The current list is shown on page 2. Handbooks for FirstGroup, Arriva and Stagecoach are also published annually. This book lists the operators that operate services during the Summer 2002 timetable and details all the vehicles in National Express colours that are used on these services. Several of the seasonal routes use vehicles in operator's own colours and, as the vehicles may vary, only the route information is given.

euroLines operations are also included where the route is contracted to an operator based in the UK or Eire. An index for National Express and euroLines services is given at the back of the book along with an index to the contracted vehicles.

Quality photographs for inclusion in the series are welcome and a fee is payable. The publishers unfortunately cannot accept responsibility for any loss and request you show your name on each picture or slide.

To keep the fleet information up to date we recommend the Ian Allan publication, **Buses** published monthly, or for more detailed information, the PSV Circle monthly news sheets.

The writer and publisher would be glad to hear from readers should any information be available which corrects or enhances that given in this publication.

Series Editor: Bill Potter
Principal Editor for *The National Express Handbook*: **Bill Potter**

Acknowledgments:
We are grateful to National Express and euroLines management, Stephen Byrne, David Donati, Keith Grimes, Mike Lambden, Colin Lloyd, the PSV Circle and the operating companies for their assistance in the compilation of this book. The cover photograph is by Tony Wilson as are both rear cover pictures. The fronticepiece is by John Marsh.

Earlier editions of the National Express Bus Handbook:
1st Edition - 2000- ISBN 1-897990-56-1

ISBN 1 897990 58 8 (Second Edition)
Published by *British Bus Publishing Ltd*
The Vyne, 16 St Margaret's Drive, Wellington, Telford, TF1 3PH

Telephone: 01952 255669 - Facsimile 01952 222397 - www.britishbuspublishing.co.uk
© British Bus Publishing Ltd, September 2002

NATIONAL EXPRESS

National Express Ltd, 4 Vicarage Road, Edgbaston, Birmingham, B15 3ES

The Early Days

Although stagecoaches were undoubtedly the forerunners of the present long distance coach network it was not until after the First World War and the introduction of motorbuses that express coach services really came into their own.

In 1919, Elliott Bros., whose coaches carried the famous 'Royal Blue' fleet name, and who had actually run one of the earlier horse drawn services, introduced a limited form of express coach service operating between Bournemouth and London.

However, Greyhound Motors of Bristol are generally acknowledged as being the first to introduce a daily, all year round, motorised express coach service in Britain. Their service, introduced in 1925, linked Bristol with London and expanded rapidly. Many other operators, able to see the commercial benefits of long distance travel, introduced similar services in the following months.

Following the establishment by NBC of the Central Activities Group in April 1972, the 'National' brand name was introduced and the now famous white livery began to appear on coaches as a first stage in offering a nationwide standard and a recognisable product to customers. The winter of 1973-74 saw the publication of the first comprehensive coach timetable that included details of the entire 'National' network. The new brand name of 'NATIONAL EXPRESS' first appeared on publicity in 1974, and on vehicles some four years later in 1978. Seen in Victoria is Duple Dominant SND282X. *Tony Wilson*

The 1930 Road Traffic Act introduced a system of licensing that covered drivers, conductors and the routes that were operated. The introduction of the Act successfully brought order to a chaotic, rapidly growing, and somewhat haphazard industry. Intending bus and coach operators now found it much harder to introduce new services, with each application for a new or revised service requiring a lengthy application to the local government appointed Traffic Commissioner. This new system of licensing provided the stability for expansion and early co-operation amongst coach operators gave rise to the formation of the first networks of co-ordinated services.

These 'Pool' networks greatly increased travel opportunities for the rapidly growing number of coach passengers. Two of the most famous coaching 'Pools' were Associated Motorways, based at Cheltenham, and London Coastal Coaches, based at the new Victoria Coach Station. Opened in 1932, the new coach station replaced the original 'London' terminus in Lupus Street, which had opened in 1924.

A New Era Dawns

The steady increase in the numbers of coach passengers peaked in the late 50's followed by a gradual decline due to the increase in the number of private cars. In 1959 the opening of the first stretches of Britain's new motorway network brought new opportunities for coach operators such as 'Midland Red' of Birmingham and 'Ribble' of Preston including the 'Gay Hostess' double deck coaches.

By the late sixties most bus companies, with the exception of municipal and small independent operators, had formed into two main groups, the state owned Tilling Group and the British Electric Traction Group (BET). In March 1968, the government brought both groups together under the Transport Holding Company.

The 1968 Transport Act brought about an integrated public passenger transport system across the country. One of the major provisions of the Act was the formation, on 28 November 1968, of the National Bus Company (NBC). NBC began operating on 1 January 1969 and, by 31 December 1969, NBC controlled 93 bus companies grouped into 44 operating units employing 81,000 staff and having a fleet of 21,000 vehicles. A new era of public transport had arrived.

Network developments

From the beginning, the directors of what was the biggest road passenger transport operation in Europe began to bring together the coaching activities of each constituent operator. The reasons were obvious. Each local company was pursuing its own policy of express coach service operation.

Inevitably this was leading to duplication of services and it was soon decided that a co-ordinated policy of express coach service planning would be of benefit to both the customer and the National Bus Company alike.

However regulation of services prevented any real expansion of services or the provision of routes where there were mass markets.

The 'National' brand name was introduced during 1972 and the original 'all white' livery began to appear on coaches as a first stage in offering customers a nationwide standard and a recognisable product. The winter of 1973/74 saw the publication of the first comprehensive coach timetable that included details of the entire 'National' network.

The new brand name, National Express, first appeared on publicity in 1974 and on vehicles in 1978. It was during at this time that the 'EXTRA' computer reservations system was also brought into operation giving an improved service to customers and booking agents by speeding up ticket issues.

In 1979, NBC commissioned a major programme of market research called 'Coachmap'. Every passenger on every journey was asked where, when and why he or she was travelling. The substantial amount of information obtained gave a much-needed insight into the travel requirements of both young and old but was never actually implemented as the 1980 Transport Act altered the whole of the network.

Deregulation and expansion

The introduction, on 6 October, of the 1980 Transport Act, swept away 50 years of licensing restrictions and introduced competition on long distance coach routes.

National Express, and the main Scottish express coach operator, Scottish Citylink, faced new competition from a host of established bus and coach operators trying their hand at operating regular long distance coach services. It came as no surprise to National Express to discover that many of the 'new' operators seemed to only want to run coaches at the busiest times. The future of the nationwide coach network, and of National Express itself, was in jeopardy.

Totally without subsidy, and by introducing new services and lower fares, National Express fought to win or perish in the ensuing war. Most of the new operators were unable to sustain continued viable operation and withdrew from operating their services within a matter of months. Even the co-operative venture mounted countrywide under the title 'British Coachways' failed to capture sufficient business.

The strengths of the nationwide, co-ordinated network operated by National Express became all too apparent and the publicity surrounding the, coach war' gave a major boost to the long-term fortunes of National Express. Customers also benefitted from the new services and lower fares and the skirmish gave National Express valuable experience that was to prove useful in the years to come. Most importantly National Express was free to provide coach services wherever it felt that there was a market.

The introduction of 'Rapide'

With skillful marketing and an eye for the needs of the customer, a handful of independent coach operators fared better than most. Both 'Trathens' from the West Country and 'Cotters' from Scotland (later to become Stagecoach) introduced up-market services operated by coaches carrying hostesses, refreshments and toilets.

Seeing the opportunities that such an operation would present on other services, National Express entered into an agreement with Trathens to co-operate in running the West Country services. This new concept of improved customer care and service quality was given the name 'Rapide'. The Rapide service introduced a hostess/steward service of light refreshments to each seat. The coaches used on the service were fitted with their own toilet/washroom, air suspension and reclining seats. The on-board facilities cut out the need for time consuming refreshment and toilet stops offering an instant saving, in journey times, of around 20%.

Public demand for the new Rapide services was high and brought about the introduction of a new design of double-deck coach to cater for the higher number of customers discovering the many benefits of coach travel for the first time.

The demand for this on-board catering was seen to be declining in the late 1990's with on-board customer surveys showing that customers were choosing to bring their own style of refreshments with them for their journey. This, coupled with improvements to catering outlets at key coach and bus stations, resulted in a gradual withdrawal of this facility over a number of years. The on-board catering facility on the few remaining National Express services to offer this service were withdrawn at the start of the 2001 Summer timetable. However it still remains in place on all Flightlink services as an additional benefit to the airport customer.

The provision of on-board washroom/toilet facilities on all National Express coach services meant that in many cases the running time of these service was unaffected by the change.

Annual passenger figures for the nationwide express coach network increased from 8.5 million in 1979 to around 15 million in 1986 as a direct result of post-deregulation competition. Today, the annual figure is around 13.5 million and is showing a small but steady annual growth. The main difference now is that the summer peaks that were experienced on some of the more popular services have now disappeared and coach services are now much busier throughout the whole of the year.

'National Express' is born

On 26 October 1986, following the introduction of the 1985 Transport Act there was deregulation within the industry to all local bus services. Although designed to increase competition between all bus and coach operators there was surprisingly little change in the long distance express coach market; itself deregulated back in 1980.

However, of greater importance to National Express was the requirement that the National Bus Company should be sold into the Private Sector. The first subsidiary, 'National Holidays' was sold in July 1986; the last, 'London Country (North East)' in April 1988.

National Express itself was the subject of a management buy-out, led by Clive Myers, on 17 March 1988. Between 1988 and 1991, National Express Holdings Ltd, the name of the company set up to buy National Express from the National Bus Company, acquired the established North Wales bus and coach operator, 'Crosville Wales'. the Merseyside based coach operator, Amberline'. the ATL Holdings Group (which included the Carlton PSV vehicle dealership and the Yelloway Trathen bus and coach company mentioned earlier) and the express coach services of Stagecoach Holdings Ltd based in Perth. It was during this period that National Express, Plaxtons and Volvo created a new purpose built coach, the Expressliner, which was unveiled on 20th March, 1989. The Expressliner, with a 'kneeling' suspension and many other features unique to National Express, brought a new standard high quality to coach travel across all routes, and today there are over 300 of its successors operating on routes across Britain.

A Highland 'fling'

The acquisition of the express coach services of the Stagecoach Holdings Group on 31 July, 1989, came at the same time as the long-standing agreement with Scottish Citylink coaches on joint operation across the English/Scottish border came to an end.

To market the new Scottish network, 'Caledonian Express' was introduced as a new brand. The Caledonian Express offices were based at the old Stagecoach premises at Walnut Grove in Perth. Tied in to the main National Express network, Caledonian Express began to grow immediately. New double-deck coaches entered service on the prestige Rapide services linking London with Scotland and new marketing initiatives were introduced offering a high quality of coach service to Scotland for the first time.

In 1993 National Express Group acquired Scottish Citylink. This acquisition enabled the Group to offer a truly 'national' coach network with services operating throughout England, Scotland and Wales. However, in August 1998, following the award in April of the franchise to operate ScotRail, Scotland's national railway, National Express Group disposed of Scottish Citylink to Metroline in a deal which left the operation intact but guaranteed the continuation of cross-border travel, using both companies' services, to experience a seamless journey.

Two of these, Trathens from the West Country and Cotters from Scotland had introduced up-market coaches equipped with hostesses, refreshments and toilets. This type of service was similar to that offered by, amongst others, Standerwick prior to their becoming part of the National Bus Company. In 1981, National Express entered into an agreement with Trathens to co-operate in the running of the West Country services to this higher specification and this standard of service quality was given the name 'Rapide'. Pictured at the Battersea parking area in 1986, C221CWW illustrates the then latest generation of double-decks, the Plaxton Paramount 4000, seen here on a Neoplan N722 underframe. *Tony Wilson*

Coaches can 'float'

Throughout its long and varied history, National Express has faced many changes. On 23 July 1991, a consortium made up of a number of City investment companies and the Drawlane Transport Group bought out National Express Holdings Ltd.

The chairman of the Drawlane Transport Group, Ray McEnhill, moved from that position and became the Chief Executive of the new company, the National Express Group Limited. Crosville Wales and Amberline were not included in the deal.

On December 1st, 1992, National Express took another change of direction when Chief Executive Ray McEnhill and deputy chief executive Adam Mills led National Express Group on to the Stock Market through the London Stock Exchange at a share price of 165p.

The prospectus issued at the time of the flotation made the Group's new strategy for development clear. Its objectives were to refocus and improve the profitability of the core coach business, develop new products and services within its existing operations and acquire new businesses in the passenger transport market. On March 23rd, 1993, National Express Group PLC sold its coach dealership, Carlton PSV Ltd leaving, as the main subsidiaries, National Express Ltd, euroLines (UK) Ltd, and the recently acquired Speedlink Airport Services Ltd.

Group Growth

The National Express Group's stated policy was to further expand the group by acquisitions within associated areas of the travel industry. This expansion took place not only in the UK but also within Europe and overseas

During 1993 the group started these purchases with one of the first major acquisitions being the Amsterdam based company, euroLines Nederland BV, which helped to strengthen the growing euroLines network of European coach services. In the UK this was quickly followed with a successful bid for East Midlands Airport.

The press release at the time stated '...the acquisition of East Midlands Airport offers growth opportunities in a related area of business where National Express can apply its passenger handling and transport expertise.' Bids for other UK airports followed resulting in the purchase of Bournemouth International Airport.

The merger of National Express with West Midlands Travel, one of Europe's largest urban bus operations based in Birmingham, and the acquisition of Taybus Holdings, a Dundee based bus company, ensured that the group had interests within the UK Bus Industry.

The privatisation of the UK rail industry meant that the National Express Group expanded even further during 1996 with the acquisition of both the Gatwick Express and Midland Main Line franchises offering development for the group in yet another mode of public transport.

Early in 1997 the Group acquired three more rail companies – North London Railways (Soon to be renamed SilverLink), Central Trains and Scotrail making it one of the largest UK rail operators.

Overseas development during 1998/9 included the acquisition of a number of American School Bus operations including the Crabtree Harman Corporation, Robinson Bus Service and Durham Transportation which put NEG into the position of one of the top three US school bus operators, with over 1,750 vehicles operating daily.

Meanwhile on the other side of the world in Australia the Group were also acquiring bus operations in Melbourne, Brisbane, Sydney & Perth, with additional rail/bus operations in Melbourne and the State of Victoria. A truly global transport Group.

As a result of these developments, the National Express Group has now become a leading mass passenger transport services company – with over 1 billion passenger journeys being made on its range of services worldwide during 2000.

Coach moves

Within the UK the Coach Division of the National Express Group, comprising National Express Ltd, Airlinks and euroLines UK/NL, were also on the acquisition trail developing new business with a number of new investments including ticketing technology and major coach station improvements.

During 1994 the first purpose built coach station to be constructed in Britain for over 25 years was opened in Norton Street, Liverpool. This new facility, which was widely acclaimed, greatly increased the number of customers using National Express services from that area.

Similar increases in passenger numbers were to be seen when new coach stations were opened by National Express at Leeds in 1996, Southampton in 1998 and Manchester during the Spring of 2002. Detailed discussions are also taking place with the local council in Birmingham to offer coach station improvements to customers in the Birmingham area.

Improvements have also been made to assist customers who want to find out about National Express services and make credit card bookings by phone and via the internet. A new Customer Contact Centre opened by the Minister of Transport John Spellar in July 2001, based in central Birmingham, offers our customers the very latest in Call Centre Technology. With more staff and more telephone lines than ever before it replaces the three previous Call Centres based at Digbeth, Glasgow and Manchester. Centralising this activity on just one site will offer major benefits to customers and enable us to offer a much improved service. It will also enable us to increase the opportunities for 'remote ticketing' facilities when customers can book by phone and collect their tickets at the station prior to departure. 60 such sites are expected to open by the end of Summer 2002.

These developments, along with the development of a computerised reservation system 'EXTRA' and an automated ticketing system 'SMART' has greatly improved the efficiency of ticketing systems for both National Express and its network of over 2,500 UK agents. Website developments have also been dramatic and are covered in the following section.

With its three main core-operating areas i.e. UK, Airport and Europe the National Express Coach Division continues to grow. Within the UK a new brand of Express Shuttle services now provide a low cost, high frequency shuttle service. First introduced in 1994 on routes between Manchester, Liverpool and Leeds they have continued to grow with routes being introduced

The internet offers passengers the chance to obtain substantial information without the need to call at booking offices. The web address gobycoach.com is managed by National Express and now promoted on vehicles. Special lettering is carried on Bebb's Y93HTX using contravison vinyl for National Express and euroLines web site, gobybus.com. The Plaxton Paragon is seen in Chesterfield.
Mark Doggett

to/from London including those from Birmingham, Brighton, Bristol, Bournemouth, Cambridge, and Southampton & Dover.

Dedicated airport coach services were also identified by National Express as an important growth area. In October 1994 a new branded service – Airlinks – specifically for the airport market, was established on the Bradford/Leeds to Heathrow/Gatwick corridor. This was followed in May 1995 with the introduction of Airlinks services on corridors between Newcastle/Nottingham to Heathrow/Gatwick, Swansea/Cardiff to Heathrow/Gatwick and Bristol to Heathrow/Gatwick. Early in 1996 the acquisition of the Flightlink brand saw the inclusion of new airport corridors from the West Midlands to Heathrow, Gatwick and Manchester airports. This was followed by the re-branding of all dedicated airport corridors to Flightlink and the launch of the Flightlink network to the retail travel trade.

In mid 1997 Speedlink Airport Services commenced operation of Hotel Hoppa, serving all 13 Heathrow airport hotels. This major operation, using 30 low floor buses was a major partnership between Speedlink, BAA and the Heathrow airport hoteliers, and succeeded in reducing traffic congestion in the Heathrow central area by over 30%.

Following a decision made in mid 1998 to bring together the airport operations of Speedlink Airport Services Ltd and the NEL airport services brand of Flightlink, a new company was formed on 1 January 1999 – AirLinks, The Airport Coach Company Limited which was to focus on airport scheduled and contract bus and coach services. Operating vehicles with distinctive liveries such as Flightlink, Speedlink, Airbus and Jetlink, the airport coach service network continues to grow. AirLinks has acquired all 3rd party interests in the Jetlink brand, acquired Silverwing Transport Services, Cambridge Coach Services Ltd, Airbus and Capital Logistics, all of which now provide coach and bus operations within the Stansted, Luton, Heathrow and Gatwick airports. AirLinks is now the largest operator of both scheduled and contract services to BAA and the airline operators.

GoByCoach

National Express were one of the first UK travel companies to recognise the importance of the internet for customers wishing to obtain both travel information and to book travel tickets – at any time of the day, and from anywhere in the world!

The GoByCoach.com website now handles over 150,000 page views per day – and has already been awarded a 'Web-site of the Week' title by The Guardian. The website address is now prominently featured on all the company literature and during 2000 the GoByCoach.com website address was also included as part of the National Express coach livery, ensuring that even more customers knew where to 'click-on'!

It's clear to see that with exciting new services, 'value for money' fares, new 'state of the art' coach stations and helpful and professional staff – there's only one way to travel Around Britain – To Airports – Throughout Europe and that's to GoByCoach

ABBOTT'S

DC & CG Abbott, Auman's House, Leeming, Northallerton, DL7 9RZ

682	Mablethorpe - Bradford
685	Hemsby - Bradford

Note: No vehicles are contracted to operate in National Express colours. The vehicles used on the service are selected from the main fleet.
Details of the coaches in this fleet may be found in The Yorkshire Bus Handbook

AIRLINKS

The Airport Coach Company Ltd, Sipson Road, West Drayton, UB7 0HN

010	London - Cambridge (from 12 August)
025	London - Brighton
027	London - Chichester
707	Milton Keynes - Heathrow
717	Brighton - Heathrow
727	Norwich -Brighton
737	Ipswich - Heathrow
757	Cambridge - Oxford
767	Cambridge - Oxford
787	Cambridge - Brighton
797	Cambridge - Brighton
A5	Victoria - Gatwick Airport
A6	Victoria - Stansted Airport
A7	Victoria - Stansted Airport
Railair Link	Heathrow Airport - Woking
Speedlink	Heathrow Airport - Gatwick Airport

D12	N21ARC	DAF DE33WSSB3000	Plaxton Première 350	C49FT	1996	Skill's, Nottingham, 2000
V40	N40SLK	Volvo B10M-62	Plaxton Première 350	C49FT	1996	Skill's, Nottingham, 2000
V50	N50SLK	Volvo B10M-62	Plaxton Première 350	C49FT	1996	Skill's, Nottingham, 2000
V60	N60SLK	Volvo B10M-62	Plaxton Première 350	C49FT	1996	Skill's, Nottingham, 2000
V70	N70SLK	Volvo B10M-62	Plaxton Première 350	C49FT	1996	Skill's, Nottingham, 2000
V80	N80SLK	Volvo B10M-62	Plaxton Première 350	C49FT	1996	Skill's, Nottingham, 2000
V90	N90SLK	Volvo B10M-62	Plaxton Première 350	C49FT	1996	Skill's, Nottingham, 2000
930	S930ATO	Dennis Javelin	Plaxton Première 320	C49FT	1998	Skill's, Nottingham, 2000

Details of the other coaches and Airlinks buses in this fleet may be found in The South East Bus Handbook.

National Express subsidiary Airlinks operate express services in the London area principally providing supporting services for the city's five airports. While only eight Plaxton Premiére 350s are in National Express colours many other coaches carry Jetlink and Speedlink liveries for these airport links. Seen in Dorking heading for Stansted, Y311HUA shows the latest Jetlink livery. *Dave Heath*

AMBASSADOR TRAVEL

Ambassador Travel Ltd, James Watt Close, Gapton Hall, Great Yarmouth, NR31 0NX

308	Great Yarmouth - Birmingham
420	London - Birmingham
495	London - Cromer
496	London - Cromer
497	London - Great Yarmouth

141	M743KJU	Volvo B10M-62	Plaxton Premiére 350	C51F	1995	
148	P411MDT	Volvo B10M-62	Plaxton Premiére 350	C48FT	1997	
149	P412MDT	Volvo B10M-62	Plaxton Premiére 350	C46FT	1997	
151	R85DVF	Volvo B10M-62	Plaxton Premiére 350	C51F	1998	
193	M35KAX	Volvo B10M-62	Plaxton Premiére 350	C49FT	1995	Bebb, Llantwit Fardre, 1997
194	240FRH	Volvo B10M-62	Plaxton Premiére 350	C49FT	1994	Bebb, Llantwit Fardre, 1998
195	P803BLJ	Volvo B10M-62	Plaxton Premiére 350	C49FT	1997	Excelsior, Bournemouth, 2001

ANDERSONS

E M & P Anderson, Hunslet Business Park, 76 Goodwin Street, Leeds, LS10 1NY

380	Bradford - Birmingham
561	Bradford - London
660	Bradford - Skegness

No vehicles operate in National Express colours. The vehicles used on the service are selected from the main fleet.

APPLEGATES

F Applegate, Heathfield Garage, Newport, Berkeley, Gloucester, GL13 9LP

040	Bristol - London
318	Bristol - Birmingham

No vehicles are contracted to operate in National Express colours. The vehicles used on the service are selected from the main fleet. Details of the coaches in this fleet may be found in The South West Bus Handbook

ARRIVA FOX COUNTY

Arriva Fox County Ltd, PO Box 613, Melton Road, Thurmaston, Leicester, LE4 8ZN

348	Leicester - Swansea
397	Leicester - Blackpool
440	London - Buxton - Leicester
440	London - Burton-on-Trent
440	London - Derby

3201	P201RWR	DAF DE33WSSB3000	Van Hool Alizée	C51FT	1997	First Edinburgh, 2001
3205	P205RWR	DAF DE33WSSB3000	Van Hool Alizée	C51FT	1997	Arriva Yorkshire, 2000
3209	T209XVO	DAF DE33WSSB3000	Van Hool T9 Alizée	C51FT	1999	
3210	T119AUA	DAF DE33WSSB3000	Van Hool T9 Alizée	C51FT	1999	
3211	662NKR	Volvo B10M-62	Plaxton Expressliner 2	C49FT	1996	
3212	N212TBC	Volvo B10M-62	Plaxton Expressliner 2	C49FT	1996	

Previous Registration

662NKR	N211TBC

Details of the other vehicles in this fleet may be found in the annual Arriva Bus Handbook

ARRIVA NORTH EAST

Arriva North East Ltd, Arriva House, Admiral Way, Sunderland, SR3 3XP

024	Eastbourne - London	
326	Cambridge - Newcastle	
425	London - Ashington	
425	London - Newcastle	

136	WSV570	Bova FHD12.290	Bova Futura	C44FT	1993
137	WSV571	Bova FHD12.290	Bova Futura	C44FT	1993
138	WSV572	Bova FHD12.290	Bova Futura	C44FT	1993
140	M122UUB	Bova FHD12.290	Bova Futura	C46FT	1993
141	V141EJR	DAF DE33WSSB3000	Van Hool T9 Alizée	C44FT	1999
142	V142EJR	DAF DE33WSSB3000	Van Hool T9 Alizée	C44FT	1999
143	X143WNL	DAF DE33WSSB3000	Van Hool T9 Alizée	C49FT	2000
144	X144WNL	DAF DE33WSSB3000	Van Hool T9 Alizée	C49FT	2000

Previous Registrations:

WSV570	L766YTN		
WSV571	L767YTN	WSV572	L768YTN

Details of the other vehicles in this fleet may be found in the annual Arriva Bus Handbook

After many years of using Bova Futura coaches on National Express duties Arriva North East have chosen the latest Van Hool Alizée style, though again based on DAF units, for which Arriva Bus and Coach are the principal British dealer. Seen in Gateshead is 143, X143WNL. *Tony Wilson*

ARRIVA YORKSHIRE

Arriva Yorkshire West Ltd, Mill Street East, Dewsbury, West Yorkshire, WF12 9AG

240		Gatwick Airport - Bradford			
240		Heathrow Airport - Bradford			
31	P31XUG	DAF DE33WSSB3000	Van Hool Alizée HE	C44FT	1997
33	A1YBG	DAF DE33WSSB3000	Van Hool T9 Alizée	C44FT	1999
34	A2YBG	DAF DE33WSSB3000	Van Hool T9 Alizée	C44FT	1999
35	A4YBG	DAF DE33WSSB3000	Van Hool T9 Alizée	C44FT	1999
36	T36EUA	DAF DE33WSSB3000	Van Hool T9 Alizée	C44FT	1999
37	T37EUA	DAF DE33WSSB3000	Van Hool T9 Alizée	C44FT	1999
38	T38EUA	DAF DE33WSSB3000	Van Hool T9 Alizée	C44FT	1999

Details of the other vehicles in this fleet may be found in the annual Arriva Bus Handbook

ASTONS

Astons of Kempsey (Coaches) Ltd, Clerken Leap, Broomhall, Worcester, WR5 3HR

euroLines services to Barcelona

	24TAE	Scania L94IB4	Van Hool Alizée II	C51FT	1999

Previous Registrations:
24TAE   T704XUY

Flightlink colours are now worn by approximately sixty coaches that are employed on services connecting with Heathrow, Stansted, Luton or Gatwick. All of Arriva Yorkshire's complement of DAF coaches are in this scheme exhibited here on T36EUA. *Tony Wilson*

BEBB

Bebb Travel plc, The Coach Station, Llantwit Fardre, Rhondda Cynon Taff, CF38 2HB

320	Cardiff - Bradford
321	Pontypridd - Bradford
509	London - Aberdare
509	London - Cardiff
536	Aberdeen - Cardiff

40	CN51XNU	Volvo B12M	Plaxton Paragon	C49FT	2002
41	CN51XNV	Volvo B12M	Plaxton Paragon	C49FT	2002
42	CN51XNW	Volvo B12M	Plaxton Paragon	C49FT	2002
43	CN51XNX	Volvo B12M	Plaxton Paragon	C49FT	2002
44	CN51XNY	Volvo B12M	Plaxton Paragon	C49FT	2002
45	CN51XNZ	Volvo B12M	Plaxton Paragon	C49FT	2002
X46	X46CNY	Volvo B10M-62	Plaxton Paragon	C49FT	2001
X47	X47CNY	Volvo B10M-62	Plaxton Paragon	C49FT	2001
X48	X48CNY	Volvo B10M-62	Plaxton Paragon	C49FT	2001
Y93	Y93HTX	Volvo B10M-62	Plaxton Paragon	C49FT	2001
Y94	Y94HTX	Volvo B10M-62	Plaxton Paragon	C49FT	2001
Y96	Y96HTX	Volvo B10M-62	Plaxton Paragon	C49FT	2001
Y97	Y97HTX	Volvo B10M-62	Plaxton Paragon	C49FT	2001

Details of the other vehicles in this fleet may be found in The Welsh Bus Handbook

The arrival of a further six Plaxton Paragon coaches on the latest Euro III-compliant Volvo B12M chassis for duties operated by Bebb has seen this body type now become standard. Special promotional livery for the Great Ormond Street Hospital is carried on Paragon Y96HTX pictured in Cardiff at the end of a journey from London. Route 536 links the Welsh capital with Aberdeen, a journey of some 880 Km. *Gerry Mead*

BIRMINGHAM COACH COMPANY

Birmingham Coach Co Ltd, Cross Quays Business Park, Hallbridge Way, Tividale, B69 3HW

325	Birmingham - Manchester
387	Blackpool - Coventry
412	Great Malvern - London
420	London - Wolverhampton
420	London - Aberystwyth
420	London - Birmingham
656	Burnham - Wolverhampton
777	Birmingham - Stansted

M441BDM	Volvo B10M-62	Plaxton Expressliner 2	C44FT	1995	
M67LAG	Scania K113CRB	Van Hool Alizée HE	C49FT	1995	
N170AAG	Scania K113CRB	Van Hool Alizée HE	C44FT	1996	East Yorkshire, 1999
N171AAG	Scania K113CRB	Van Hool Alizée HE	C44FT	1996	East Yorkshire, 1999
N172AAG	Scania K113CRB	Van Hool Alizée HE	C44FT	1996	East Yorkshire, 1999
N173AAG	Scania K113CRB	Van Hool Alizée HE	C44FT	1996	East Yorkshire, 1999
N369TJT	Scania K113CRB	Van Hool Alizée HE	C49FT	1996	Dorset Travel, 2001
N370TJT	Scania K113CRB	Van Hool Alizée HE	C49FT	1996	Dorset Travel, 2001
X421WVO	Scania K124IB4	Van Hool T9 Alizée	C44FT	2001	
X422WVO	Scania K124IB4	Van Hool T9 Alizée	C44FT	2001	
X423WVO	Scania K124IB4	Van Hool T9 Alizée	C44FT	2001	
YP02AAV	Scania K114IB4	Van Hool T9 Alizée	C49FT	2002	
YP02AAX	Scania K114IB4	Van Hool T9 Alizée	C49FT	2002	

M441BDM is owned by National Express and operated by Birmingham Coach Company on behalf of National Express. Details of the other vehicles in this fleet may be found in the West Midlands Bus Handbook.

Scania is the preferred chassis for coaches operated by The Birmingham Coach Company, and all have Van Hool Alizée bodywork. Seen leaving the now refurbished Chorlton Street bus station in Manchester is X421WVO. *Mark Doggett*

BOURNEMOUTH TRANSPORT

Bournemouth Transport Ltd, Transport Depot, Mallard Road, Bournemouth, BH8 9PN

032	Bournemouth - London
032	Plymouth - Southampton - London
035	Poole - London
652	Southampton - London

319	R319NRU	Volvo B10M-62	Berkhof Axial 50	C49FT	1998
324	W324UEL	Volvo B10M-62	Berkhof Axial 50	C49FT	1999
326	R326NRU	Volvo B10M-62	Van Hool T9 Alizée	C49FT	1998
327	R327NRU	Volvo B10M-62	Van Hool T9 Alizée	C49FT	1998
329	R329NRU	Volvo B10M-62	Van Hool T9 Alizée	C49FT	1998
330	T330AFX	Volvo B10M-62	Van Hool T9 Alizée	C49FT	1999
331	T331AFX	Volvo B10M-62	Van Hool T9 Alizée	C49FT	1999
336	Y336CJT	Volvo B10M-62	Berkhof Axial 50	C49FT	2001
350	R350LPR	Scania L94IB	Van Hool T9 Alizée	C55FT	1997
351	R351LPR	Scania L94IB	Van Hool T9 Alizée	C55FT	1997
352	P352ARU	Scania K113TRB	Van Hool Alizée HE	C49FT	1997
353	P353ARU	Scania K113TRB	Van Hool Alizée HE	C49FT	1997
354	R354NRU	Volvo B10M-62	Van Hool T9 Alizée	C49FT	1998
355	R355NRU	Volvo B10M-62	Van Hool T9 Alizée	C49FT	1998
381	W381UEL	Scania L94IB	Van Hool T9 Alizée	C49FT	2000
382	W382UEL	Scania L94IB	Van Hool T9 Alizée	C49FT	2000
383	W383UEL	Scania L94IB	Van Hool T9 Alizée	C49FT	2000
384	W384UEL	Scania L94IB	Van Hool T9 Alizée	C49FT	2000

Details of the other vehicles in this fleet may be found in the South West Bus Handbook.

Shuttle livery is carried on Scania 384, W384UEL in the Bournemouth Transport fleet. This company has now acquired and absorbed the post-privatised Dorset Travel Services, the former National Express coaching unit. Shuttle livery is applied those vehicles allocated to the more frequent services.

BENNETTS OF WARRINGTON

B A Bennett, Athlone Road, Longford, Warrington, WA2 8JJ

691   Liverpool - Scarborough

No vehicles are contracted to operate in National Express colours. The vehicles used on the service are selected from the parent Holmeswood Coaches fleet. Details of the vehicle in this fleet may be found in The Lancashire, Cumbria and Manchester Bus Handbook.

BRUCE'S

J. Bruce, 40 Main Street, Salsburgh, ML7 4LA

539   Bournemouth - Edinburgh

V10NAT	Bova FHD12.340	Bova Futura	C46FT	2000
X20NAT	Bova FHD12.340	Bova Futura	C46FT	2001

BURGIN

Burgin European (Coach Hirers) Ltd, Unit 6, 35 Catley Road, Darnall, Sheffield, S9 5JF

561   Bradford - London

No vehicles are contracted to operate in National Express colours. The vehicles used on the service are selected from the main fleet.

BURTON'S

Burton's Coaches Ltd, Duddery Hill, Haverhill, Suffolk, CB9 8DR

010   London - Cambridge

No vehicles are contracted to operate in National Express colours. The vehicles used on the service are selected from the main fleet. Details of the vehicles in this fleet may be found in The Eastern Bus Handbook

BUZZLINES

Buzzlines Ltd, 61 Lympne Industrial Estate, Lympne, Hythe, CT21 4LR

| T10BUS | Setra S315 GT-HD | Setra | C48FT | 1999 |

Details of the vehicles in this fleet may be found in The South East Bus Handbook

CASTLE COACHES

Castle Coaches Ltd, 5 Queens Crescent, Waterlooville, PO8 9NB

| 668 | London - Bognor |

No vehicles are contracted to operate in National Express colours. The vehicles used on the service are selected from the main fleet.

A new design of coach, the National Expressliner, was introduced in March 1989 in a joint venture between Volvo, Plaxton and National Express. The Expressliner was designed to be the standard express coach for the network and to be available to all operating companies. Initially fitted to Rapide specification it included many features aimed at improving passenger comfort, convenience and safety. One of the first generation of Expressliners is J917LEM pictured in Durham while operating with Selwyn's on route 83 linking north east Wales with Edinburgh. *Tony Wilson*

CHALFONT

Chalfont Coaches of Harrow Ltd, 200 Featherstone Road, Southall, UB2 5AQ

040	London - Bristol	560	London - Sheffield
412	London - Gloucester	561	London - Leeds
440	London - Leicester	681	Birmingham - Maplethorpe
460	London - Coventry	683	Birmingham - Hemsby
505	London - Newquay		

No vehicles are contracted to operate in National Express colours. The vehicles used on the service are selected from the main fleet.

CHENERY

P G & G Chenery, The Garage, Dickleborough, Diss, Norfolk, IP21 4NJ

490	London - Great Yarmouth	490	London - Norwich
490	London - Norwich Castle		

RYG684	Setra S215HD	Setra Tornado	C44FT	1994	
R303EEX	Setra S250	Setra Special	C44FT	1998	
R304EEX	Setra S250	Setra Special	C44FT	1998	
R39AWO	Setra S250	Setra Special	C44FT	1998	Bebb, Llantwit Fardre, 2000

Details of the vehicles in this fleet may be found in The Eastern Bus Handbook.

Setra has been chosen by Bebb for its National Express duties on several occasions, and one of their former vehicles was added to the Chenery complement in 2000 when displaced in south Wales. July 2002 saw R39AWO on Millbank in London while working a short service to Thetford. *Tony Wilson*

COUNTRY TRAVEL

M Patrick, Moores Yard, Benhall, Saxmundham, IP17 1HB

497   London – Great Yarmouth

No vehicles are contracted to operate in National Express colours. The vehicles used on the service are selected from the main fleet.

DON SMITH

D A Smith & S A Reekie, 4 The Croft, Murton, SR7 9PB

426   Sunderland - London

No vehicles are contracted to operate in National Express colours. The vehicles used on the service are selected from the main fleet.

While many operators provide daily services using coaches in National Express colours, other operators have contracts for journeys less frequent, often at the weekend, and for which they use vehicles in their own colours, and thus it not possible to show the selected vehicles in this list. Recently displaced by Bebb, is luxury coach V35HAX, a Setra 315GT and one of only three to carry National Express colours. *Tony Wilson*

DUNN-LINE

Dunn-Line Holdings Ltd, The Coach Station, Park Lane, Basford, Nottingham, NG6 0DW

329	St. Ives - Nottingham
330	Birmingham - Nottingham
450	Mansfield - London

S295WOA	Volvo B10M-66SE	Plaxton Expressliner 2	C44FT	1999	Flights, Birmingham, 2002
S296WOA	Volvo B10M-66SE	Plaxton Expressliner 2	C44FT	1999	Flights, Birmingham, 2002
S297WOA	Volvo B10M-66SE	Plaxton Expressliner 2	C44FT	1998	Flights, Birmingham, 2002
S298WOA	Volvo B10M-66SE	Plaxton Expressliner 2	C44FT	1998	Flights, Birmingham, 2002
S364OOB	Volvo B10M-66SE	Plaxton Expressliner 2	C44FT	1998	Flights, Birmingham, 2002
S365OOB	Volvo B10M-66SE	Plaxton Expressliner 2	C44FT	1998	Flights, Birmingham, 2002
V447EAL	Volvo B10M-62	Plaxton Expressliner 2	C44FT	1999	Flights, Birmingham, 2002
V448EAL	Volvo B10M-62	Plaxton Expressliner 2	C44FT	1999	Flights, Birmingham, 2002
V449EAL	Volvo B10M-62	Plaxton Expressliner 2	C44FT	1999	Flights, Birmingham, 2002
A8FTG	Volvo B10M-66SE	Plaxton Excalibur	C44FT	2000	Flight's, Birmingham, 2002

Details of the vehicles in this fleet may be found in The East Midlands Bus Handbook

Dunn-Line have recently acquired Flight's operations and now are the principal suppliers of vehicles for three routes. The Expressliner II was a similarly modified Plaxton coach to the initial Expressliner but based on the Premiere 350. S297WOA is seen in Wolverhampton. *Mark Doggett*

DURHAM TRAVEL

Durham Travel Services Ltd, Byron House, Seaham Grange, Co Durham, SR7 0PW

380	Newcastle - Leeds
426	London - South Shields
460	London - Lichfield
481	London - Felixstowe
561	London - Bradford
561	London - Keighley
561	London - Knaresborough
561	London - Ripon
561	London - Skipton
563	London - Whitby
591	London - Edinburgh

19	M131HJR	Scania K113CRB	Van Hool Alizée	C44FT	1995
22	N22DTS	Volvo B10M-66SE	Plaxton Expressliner 2	C44FT	1995
23	N23RTN	Volvo B10M-66SE	Plaxton Expressliner 2	C44FT	1996
24	P24WNL	Volvo B10M-66SE	Plaxton Expressliner 2	C44FT	1996
26	S26DTS	Scania K124IB4	Van Hool Alizée II	C44FT	1999
27	S27DTS	Scania K124IB4	Van Hool Alizée II	C44FT	1999
28	L28ABB	Scania K113CRB	Van Hool Alizée	C44FT	1994
30	W30DTS	Scania K124IB4	Van Hool Alizée	C44FT	2000
31	W431RBB	Scania K124IB4	Van Hool Alizée	C44FT	2000
32	W432RBB	Scania K124IB4	Van Hool Alizée	C44FT	2000
33	NK51ORJ	Scania K124IB4	Van Hool T9 Alizée	C49FT	2001
34	NK51ORL	Scania K124IB4	Van Hool T9 Alizée	C49FT	2001
35	NK51ORN	Scania K124IB4	Van Hool T9 Alizée	C49FT	2001
36	NK51ORO	Scania K124IB4	Van Hool T9 Alizée	C49FT	2001
37	M37HJR	Scania K113CRB	Van Hool Alizée	C49FT	1995
38	M38HJR	Scania K113CRB	Van Hool Alizée	C49FT	1995
39	M39HJR	Scania K113CRB	Van Hool Alizée	C49FT	1995
56	P56XNL	Volvo B10M - 66SE	Plaxton Expressliner 2	C44FT	1996
57	P57XNL	Volvo B10M - 66SE	Plaxton Expressliner 2	C44FT	1996

Details of the vehicles in this fleet may be found in The North East Bus Handbook

There is no excuse for not seeing the telephone number for National Express bookings as Durham Travel's 19, M131HJR, passes by. The vehicle is a Scania K113 with Van Hool Alizée bodywork. Durham Travel has a similar history to Dorset Travel having been created to tender for National Express contracts as its core business with other coaching work as could be developed. Subsequent growth has seen this operator join the ranks of London Bus operators. *Dave Heath*

EAST YORKSHIRE

East Yorkshire Motor Services Ltd, 252 Anlaby Road, Hull, HU3 2RS

322	Hull - Swansea	
322	Brecon - Scarborough	
390	Manchester - Hull	
562	London - Hull	
562	London - Beverley	

37	P837XAG	Volvo B10M-62	Plaxton Première 350	C44FT	1997
38	V838JAT	Volvo B10M-60	Plaxton Expressliner 2	C49FT	2000
39	V839JAT	Volvo B10M-60	Plaxton Expressliner 2	C49FT	2000
40	V840JAT	Volvo B10M-60	Plaxton Expressliner 2	C49FT	2000
41	V841JAT	Volvo B10M-60	Plaxton Expressliner 2	C49FT	2000
42	V842JAT	Volvo B10M-60	Plaxton Expressliner 2	C49FT	2000
43	V843JAT	Volvo B10M-60	Plaxton Expressliner 2	C49FT	2000
44	W844SKH	Volvo B10M-60	Plaxton Expressliner 2	C44FT	2000
45	Y445XAT	Volvo B	Plaxton Paragon	C49FT	2000
46	YX02JFY	Volvo B12M	Plaxton Paragon	C49FT	2002

Details of the vehicles in this fleet may be found in The Yorkshire Bus Handbook

Pictured at the London end of route 562 from Hull, East Yorkshire's 39, V839JAT is a Volvo B10M with Plaxton Expressliner 2 bodywork. *Dave Heath*

EXCELSIOR

Excelsior Coaches Ltd, Bournemouth Sands Hotel, West Cliff Gdns, Bournemouth, BH2 5HR

| 035 | Bournemouth - London |
| 205 | Poole - Heathrow Airport |

437	S809ORU	Volvo B10M-62	Plaxton Excalibur	C36FT	1998
805	A9XCL	Volvo B10M-62	Plaxton Paragon	C44FT	2000
901	R423LCG	Volvo B10M-62	Plaxton Excalibur	C49FT	1998
905	X852WLJ	Volvo B10M-62	Plaxton Paragon	C44FT	2000
906	A8XCL	Volvo B10M-62	Plaxton Paragon	C44FT	2000

Previous Registrations:

| R423LCG | XEL4 | | X852WLJ | A7XCL |
| S809DRU | XEL31 | | | |

Excelsior operate two Plaxton Excalibur coaches including S809DRU, seen here after gaining its new index mark following the restructuring and sale of Excelsior coaches by Flights to its new investors.
Dave Heath

Pictured in Calcot Services is SBZ3907 of Impact Travel. Unusually, the two vehicles were new with their 'dateless' Northern Ireland marks.
John Marsh

EXPRESS TRAVEL

Express Travel (Holdings) Ltd, Woodend Avenue, Speke, Liverpool, L24 9NB

060	Liverpool - Manchester
060	Liverpool - Leeds
305	Southend - Liverpool
314	Cambridge - Southport
350	Clacton-on-Sea - Liverpool
355	Birkenhead - Blackpool
664	Preston - Skegness

L705PHE	Volvo B10M-62	Van Hool Alizée HE	C46FT	1994
L707PHE	Volvo B10M-62	Van Hool Alizée HE	C46FT	1994
L708PHE	Volvo B10M-62	Van Hool Alizée HE	C46FT	1994
L709PHE	Volvo B10M-62	Van Hool Alizée HE	C46FT	1994
L710PHE	Volvo B10M-62	Van Hool Alizée HE	C46FT	1994
L711PHE	Volvo B10M-62	Van Hool Alizée HE	C46FT	1994
L712PHE	Volvo B10M-62	Van Hool Alizée HE	C46FT	1994
L713PHE	Volvo B10M-62	Van Hool Alizée HE	C46FT	1994
L714PHE	Volvo B10M-62	Van Hool Alizée HE	C46FT	1994
P842WUG	Volvo B10M-62	Van Hool Alizée HE	C50FT	1997
P251AUT	Volvo B10M-62	Jonckheere Mistral 50	C51FT	1997

Details of the vehicles in this fleet may be found in The Merseyside & Cheshire Bus Handbook

The Manchester terminus for National Express, located in Chorlton Street near Piccadilly, saw a major rebuild and, on re-opening, a new title. Now known as the Manchester Central coach station it replaced facilities that have been in use for over thirty years. Seen in adjacent Portland Street is *Shuttle*-liveried L711PHE from the Express Travel fleet. *Brian Ridgway*

FARGO

L J Smith, All Views, School Road, Rayne, Braintree, CM7 8SS

314   Cambridge - Birmingham

No vehicles are contracted to operate in National Express colours. The vehicles used on the service are selected from the main fleet.
Details of the coaches in this fleet may be found in The Eastern Bus Handbook

FIRST AVON

First Bristol Buses Ltd, Enterprise House, Easton Road, Bristol BS5 0DZ

402	London - Frome
403	London - Bath
403	London - Street

297	R297AYB	Dennis Javelin GX 12SDA2153	Plaxton Expressliner 2	C49FT	1998	
299	R299AYB	Dennis Javelin GX 12SDA2153	Plaxton Expressliner 2	C49FT	1998	
2564	TDZ3265	Volvo B10M-60	Plaxton Expressliner 2	C46FT	1993	First Wessex, 2001
2567	865GAT	Volvo B10M-60	Plaxton Expressliner 2	C46FT	1993	First Wessex, 2001
2570	WV02EUP	Volvo B12M	Plaxton Paragon Expressliner	C49FT	2002	
2571	WV02EUR	Volvo B12M	Plaxton Paragon Expressliner	C49FT	2002	
2572	WV02EUT	Volvo B12M	Plaxton Paragon Expressliner	C49FT	2002	
2573	WV02EUU	Volvo B12M	Plaxton Paragon Expressliner	C49FT	2002	

Previous Registrations:

865GAT	L67UOU		TDZ3265	L64UOU

Fleet numbers are expected to change in the Autumn of 2002. See the 2003 First Bus Handbook more information.

The First fleet based in Bristol gained DfT dispensation to operate four 12.8 metre wheelchair- accessible Volvo B12Ms with Plaxton Paragon bodies. Plaxton's parent, Transbus have received orders for twenty-one of the new coaches which are due to enter service in the coming months. The model in known as the Paragon Expressliner, rather than Expressliner III. WV02EUP is seen at London Heathrow. *Dave Heath*

FIRST CYMRU

First Cymru Ltd, Heol Gwyrosydd, Penlan, Swansea, SA5 7BN

201	Gatwick Airport - Swansea				
508	London - Swansea				
508	London - Llanelli				
508	London - Haverfordwest				
528	Birmingham - Haverfordwest				

101	T101XDE	Dennis Javelin GX	Plaxton Expressliner 2	C44FT	1999	
102	T102XDE	Dennis Javelin GX	Plaxton Expressliner 2	C44FT	1999	
103	T103XDE	Dennis Javelin GX	Plaxton Expressliner 2	C44FT	1999	
105	P804BLJ	Volvo B10M-62	Plaxton Expressliner 2	C44FT	1997	Excelsior, Bournemouth, 2000
	T948UEU	Volvo B10M-62	Plaxton Expressliner 2	C44FT	1999	First in Avon, 2002
	T64BHY	Volvo B10M-62	Plaxton Expressliner 2	C44FT	1999	First in Avon, 2002
109	M109PWN	Dennis Javelin GX 12SDA2133	Plaxton Expressliner 2	C44FT	1995	
110	M110PWN	Dennis Javelin GX 12SDA2133	Plaxton Expressliner 2	C44FT	1995	
111	M111PWN	Dennis Javelin GX 12SDA2133	Plaxton Expressliner 2	C44FT	1995	
112	N112EWJ	Dennis Javelin GX 12SDA2153	Plaxton Expressliner 2	C44FT	1996	
113	N113VWN	Dennis Javelin GX 12SDA2153	Plaxton Expressliner 2	C44FT	1996	
114	N114VWN	Dennis Javelin GX 12SDA2153	Plaxton Expressliner 2	C44FT	1996	
115	N115VWN	Dennis Javelin GX 12SDA2153	Plaxton Expressliner 2	C44FT	1996	
116	S116RKG	Dennis Javelin GX	Plaxton Expressliner 2	C44FT	1999	
175	R175VWN	Dennis Javelin GX	Plaxton Premiére 350	C44FT	1998	
176	R176VWN	Dennis Javelin GX	Plaxton Premiére 350	C44FT	1998	
177	R177VWN	Dennis Javelin GX	Plaxton Premiére 350	C44FT	1998	
178	R178VWN	Dennis Javelin GX	Plaxton Premiére 350	C44FT	1998	

Fleet numbers are expected to change in the Autumn of 2002. See the 2003 First Bus Handbook for more information.

Thirteen of the First in Cymru's coach fleet carry Flightlink colours, the exceptions being 115 and 175-178. Having arrived from London Gatwick, M109PWN is one of the Javelin models with all, bar three, are now confined to 'First' operations. *Gerry Mead*

FIRST SOMERSET & DORSET

First Southern National Ltd, 4 Hamilton Road, Taunton, TA1 2EH

040	London - Brean Sands
040	London - Bristol
050	Bristol - Cardiff
200	Bristol - Gatwick Airport
310	Birmingham - Bradford
318	Bristol - Liverpool
325	Birmingham - Manchester
341	Paignton - Burnley
420	London - Birmingham
420	London - Wolverhampton
460	London - Stratford-upon-Avon
545	London - Pwllheli

6169	M92BOU	Volvo B10M-62	Plaxton Expressliner 2	C46FT	1994
6176	M765CWS	Volvo B10M-62	Plaxton Expressliner 2	C49FT	1994
6179	M440FHW	Volvo B10M-62	Plaxton Expressliner 2	C49FT	1995
6180	M41FTC	Volvo B10M-62	Plaxton Expressliner 2	C44FT	1995
6181	P944RWS	Volvo B10M-62	Plaxton Expressliner 2	C46FT	1996
6182	P945RWS	Volvo B10M-62	Plaxton Expressliner 2	C44FT	1996
6183	P946RWS	Volvo B10M-62	Plaxton Expressliner 2	C49FT	1996
6184	R813HWS	Volvo B10M-62	Plaxton Expressliner 2	C49FT	1997
6185	R814HWS	Volvo B10M-62	Plaxton Expressliner 2	C49FT	1997
6186	R943LHT	Volvo B10M-62	Plaxton Expressliner 2	C44FT	1998
6189	T310AHY	Volvo B10M-62	Plaxton Expressliner 2	C44FT	1996
6191	X191HFB	Volvo B10M-62	Plaxton Expressliner 2	C44FT	2000
6192	X192HFB	Volvo B10M-62	Plaxton Expressliner 2	C44FT	2000
6193	X193HFB	Volvo B10M-62	Plaxton Expressliner 2	C44FT	2000
6194	X194HFB	Volvo B10M-62	Plaxton Expressliner 2	C44FT	2000

The former First Wessex operations were integrated under First Somerset and Dorset management during 2001. Seen in Birmingham's Digbeth, though lettered for the London to Bristol Shuttle is Dennis N471KHU, one of a dozen used by this fleet. First are in the process of renumbering the vehicles and this exercise is expected to be completed during the Autumn of 2002. *Mark Doggett*

6201 - 6212		Dennis Javelin 12SDA2153		Plaxton Expressliner 2		C49FT		1995-96	
6201	N471KHU	6204	N474KHU	6207	N821KWS	6209	N319NHY	6211	N321NHY
6202	N472KHU	6205	N913KHW	6208	N822KWS	6210	N320NHY	6212	N322NHY
6203	N473KHU	6206	N914KHW						

6301	WX51AJU	Volvo B12M	Plaxton Paragon	C44FT	2001	
6302	WX51AJV	Volvo B12M	Plaxton Paragon	C44FT	2001	
6303	WX51AJY	Volvo B12M	Plaxton Paragon	C44FT	2001	
6304	WX51AKY	Volvo B12M	Plaxton Paragon	C49FT	2001	

Fleet numbers are expected to change in the Autumn of 2002. See the 2003 First Bus Handbook for more information.

FIRST DEVON & CORNWALL

First Red Bus Ltd; First Western National Buses Ltd,
Western House, 38 Lemon Street, Truro, TR1 2NS

339	Grimsby - Westward Ho!	330	Penzance - Nottingham
502	London - Bideford	336	Penzance - Edinburgh
502	London - Ilfracombe	403	London - Bath Spa
502	London - Westward Ho!	404	London - Penzance
315	Heston - Eastbourne	500	London - Penzance
328	Plymouth - Rochdale	504	London - Penzance
329	St. Ives - Nottingham	505	London - Penzance
329	Bristol - Newquay		

One of the latest Paragons to carry Flightlink colours is 6302, WX51AJU seen here at rest at London Gatwick. The coach is one of four added to the First's Somerset and Dorset fleet during 2001. *Dave Heath*

Helston is the location for this view of 2310, R310JAF as it heads for London. In 1992 agreement was reached on a second generation of Expressliner, with the new model being unveiled on 23rd July. Also based on the Volvo B10M chassis it carries the later Plaxton Premiére 350 design modified to the requirements of National Express. These modifications included the solid, white, rear and double N motif and was marked as a different body type. The first three entered service with Amberline in early August 1992. All were initially built using the latest version of the B10M coach chassis, which featured an up rated 285bhp low pollution engine.
Tony Wilson

2301	M301BRL	Volvo B10M-62	Plaxton Expressliner 2	C46FT	1994	
2302	M302BRL	Volvo B10M-62	Plaxton Expressliner 2	C46FT	1994	
2303	M303BRL	Volvo B10M-62	Plaxton Expressliner 2	C46FT	1994	
2304	R304JAF	Volvo B10M-62	Plaxton Expressliner 2	C44FT	1998	
2305	R305JAF	Volvo B10M-62	Plaxton Expressliner 2	C44FT	1998	
2307	R307JAF	Volvo B10M-62	Plaxton Expressliner 2	C44FT	1998	
2308	R308JAF	Volvo B10M-62	Plaxton Expressliner 2	C44FT	1998	
2309	R309JAF	Volvo B10M-62	Plaxton Expressliner 2	C44FT	1998	
2310	R310JAF	Volvo B10M-62	Plaxton Expressliner 2	C44FT	1998	
2311	S311SCV	Volvo B10M-62	Plaxton Expressliner 2	C44FT	1998	
2312	S312SCV	Volvo B10M-62	Plaxton Expressliner 2	C44FT	1998	
2313	S313SCV	Volvo B10M-62	Plaxton Expressliner 2	C44FT	1998	
2314	S314SRL	Volvo B10M-62	Plaxton Interurban	BC51F	1999	
2315	S315SRL	Volvo B10M-62	Plaxton Interurban	BC57F	1999	
2316	T316KCV	Volvo B10M-62	Plaxton Expressliner 2	C44FT	1999	
2521	P521PRL	Volvo B10M-62	Van Hool Alizée	C44FT	1996	
2522	P522PRL	Volvo B10M-62	Van Hool Alizée	C44FT	1996	
2701	WK02UMA	Volvo B12M	Plaxton Paragon	C49FT	2002	
2702	WK02UMB	Volvo B12M	Plaxton Paragon	C49FT	2002	
2703	WK02UMC	Volvo B12M	Plaxton Paragon	C49FT	2002	
2850	N232WFJ	Dennis Javelin GX12SDA2161	Plaxton Expressliner 2	C44FT	1996	
2851	N233WFJ	Dennis Javelin GX12SDA2161	Plaxton Expressliner 2	C44FT	1996	
2852	P234BFJ	Volvo B10M-62	Plaxton Expressliner 2	C49FT	1996	
2853	P235CTA	Dennis Javelin GX12SDA2153	Plaxton Expressliner 2	C44FT	1997	
2854	P236CTA	Dennis Javelin GX12SDA2153	Plaxton Expressliner 2	C44FT	1997	
	R298AYB	Dennis Javelin GX 12SDA2153	Plaxton Expressliner 2	C49FT	1998	First in Avon, 2002

Fleet numbers are expected to change in the Autumn of 2002. See the 2003 First Bus Handbook for more information.

FOUR SQUARE

S Riggott, Three Acres, Hoyle Mill Road, Kinsley, Pontefract, WF9 5JB

310	Bradford - Leicester
329	Leeds - Newquay
381	Leeds - Newcastle
693	Leeds - Ty-Mawr

No vehicles are contracted to operate in National Express colours. The vehicles used on the service are selected from the main fleet. Details of the vehicles in this fleet may be found in The Yorkshire Bus Handbook

G & S TRAVEL

G Rimmer, 14 Pysons Road, Ramsgate, CT12 6TS

022	London - Ramsgate
655	London - Dymchurch

No vehicles are contracted to operate in National Express colours. The vehicles used on the service are selected from the main fleet.

GALLOWAY

Galloway European Coachlines Ltd, Denter's Hill, Mendlesham, Stowmarket, IP14 5RR

481	London - Felixstowe
484	London - Clacton-on-Sea
484	London - Walton-on-the-Naze

R161GNW	DAF DE33WSSB3000	Van Hool Alizée HE	C49FT	1998	Armchair, Brentford, 1999
R256FBJ	DAF DE33WSSB3000	Van Hool Alizée HE	C49FT	1998	
V215EGV	DAF DE33WSSB3000	Van Hool Alizée II	C49FT	2000	

No vehicles are contracted to operate in National Express colours. The vehicles used on the service are selected from the main fleet. Details of the vehicles in this fleet may be found in The Eastern Bus Handbook

GO - NORTHERN

Go-Ahead Group plc, 117 Queen Street, Bensham, Gateshead, NE8 2UA

304	Weymouth - Liverpool
332	Newcastle - Birmingham
380	Bangor - Liverpool - Newcastle
381	Chester - Leeds - Newcastle
530	Paignton - Newcastle
531	Plymouth - Newcastle
663	Skegness - Newcastle

7058	JCN822	Volvo B10M-60	Plaxton Expressliner 2	C46FT	1995
7059	FCU190	Volvo B10M-60	Plaxton Expressliner 2	C46FT	1995
7060	CU6860	Volvo B10M-62	Plaxton Expressliner 2	C46FT	1996
7061	CU7661	Volvo B10M-62	Plaxton Expressliner 2	C46FT	1996
7062	GSK962	Volvo B10M-62	Plaxton Expressliner 2	C44FT	1997
7074	YSU874	Volvo B10M-62	Plaxton Expressliner 2	C44FT	1997
7075	YSU875	Volvo B10M-62	Plaxton Expressliner 2	C44FT	1997
7076	YSU876	Volvo B10M-62	Plaxton Expressliner 2	C44FT	1997
7077	S977ABR	Volvo B10M-62	Plaxton Expressliner 2	C44FT	1998
7078	S978ABR	Volvo B10M-62	Plaxton Expressliner 2	C44FT	1998
7079	S979ABR	Volvo B10M-62	Plaxton Expressliner 2	C44FT	1998
7080	Y808MFT	Volvo B10M-62	Plaxton Paragon	C49FT	2001
7081	Y781MFT	Volvo B10M-62	Plaxton Paragon	C49FT	2001
7082	Y782MFT	Volvo B10M-62	Plaxton Paragon	C49FT	2001
7083	Y783MFT	Volvo B10M-62	Plaxton Paragon	C49FT	2001
7084	Y784MFT	Volvo B10M-62	Plaxton Paragon	C49FT	2001
7085	Y785MFT	Volvo B10M-62	Plaxton Paragon	C49FT	2001

Previous Registrations:

CU6860	N760RCU	FCU190	M59LBB		JCN822	M58LBB
CU7661	N761RCU	GSK962	JSK346			

Details of the vehicles in this fleet may be found in The North East Bus Handbook

Route 304, the service linking Liverpool with Weymouth, includes several towns of note. Seen in Oxford, where the Go-Ahead group are one of the main bus service providers, 7077, S977ABR, continues south.
Dave Heath

GOODES

K Goode, Farm Garage, Crankhall Lane, Wednesbury, WS10 0ED

420   London - Birmingham

No vehicles are contracted to operate in National Express colours. The vehicles used on the service are selected from the main fleet.

HARDINGS

Hardings Tours, 50 Grange Road West, Birkenhead, CH41 4DA

540   London - Manchester
570   London - Blackpool

No vehicles are contracted to operate in National Express colours. The vehicles used on the service are selected from the main fleet. Details of the coaches in this fleet may be found in The Cheshire & Merseyside Bus Handbook

Several of the operators contracted for weekend duties provide vehicles in National Express colours. One of these is Hayton's, whose P59XNL is seen leaving Manchester for London. Hayton's provide one return daily journey on the 540 with additional work at weekends. *Mark Doggett*

HAYTON

B Hayton, 12 Acorn Close, Ferguson Park, Manchester, M19 2HS

540		London - Bolton				
540		Manchester - London				
695		Manchester - Pwllheli				

59	P59XNL	Volvo B10M - 66SE	Plaxton Expressliner 2	C44FT	1996	Durham Travel, 2001

The vehicles used on the service are also selected from the main fleet.

HELLYERS

Hellyers of Fareham Ltd, Fort Fareham Business Park, Newgate Lane, Fareham, PO14 1AH

032	Southampton - London

No vehicles are contracted to operate in National Express colours. The vehicles used on the service are selected from the main fleet. Details of the coaches in this fleet may be found in The South East Bus Handbook

IMPACT TRAVEL

T Marley 1 Leighton Road, Ealing, London, W13 9EL

040	London - Bristol
450	London - Nottingham

No vehicles are contracted to operate in National Express colours. The vehicles used on the service are selected from the main fleet.

JONES INTERNATIONAL

M & M Jones, Bron-y-De, Gwynfe, Ffairfach, Llandeilo, Carmarthenshire, SA19 6UY

322	Swansea - Birmingham
672	Swansea - Minehead

No vehicles are contracted to operate in National Express colours. The vehicles used on the service are selected from the main fleet. Details of the coaches in this fleet may be found in The Welsh Bus Handbook

KMP

KMP (Llanberis) Ltd, Y Glyn Industrial Estate, Llanberis, Gwynedd, LL55 4HN

euroLines services include those to Dublin and Amsterdam

772URB	Volvo B10M-60	Plaxton Premiére 350	C49FT	1992	Excelsior, Bournemouth, 1996
6697RU	Volvo B10M-60	Plaxton Premiére 350	C49FT	1992	Excelsior, Bournemouth, 1996
7CCH	Volvo B10M-62	Plaxton Expressliner	C44FT	1994	Excelsior, Bournemouth, 1999
K7KMP	Volvo B10M-62	Jonckheere Deauville 45	C51FT	1994	Mid Wales, Penrhyncoch, 1997
M7KMP	Volvo B10M-62	Jonckheere Deauville 45	C51FT	1994	
N77KMP	Volvo B10M-62	Plaxton Premiére 350	C49FT	1996	
N777KMP	Volvo B10M-62	Plaxton Premiére 350	C49FT	1996	
A7KMP	Volvo B10M-62	Jonckheere Mistral 50	C49FT	1998	
T7KMP	Neoplan N116/3	Neoplan Cityliner	C48FT	1999	
M77KMP	Neoplan N116/3	Neoplan Cityliner	C48FT	2002	
	Neoplan N116/3	Neoplan Cityliner	C48FT	2002	

Previous Registrations; -

772URB	A18XEL, J59NJT	7CCH	M802KJT	M77KMP	M875UEJ
6697RU	A17XEL, N663THO	K7KMP	M874UEJ		

Details of the other coaches in this fleet may be found in The Welsh Bus Handbook

KINGSTONS of ESSEX

Kingstons of Essex Ltd, 11 The Hylands, Hockley, SS5 4PP

420   London - Birmingham
540   London - Manchester
684   London - Hemsby

No vehicles are contracted to operate in National Express colours. The vehicles used on the service are selected from the main fleet. Details of the vehicles in this fleet may be found in The Eastern Bus Handbook

LEONS

Leons Coach (Stafford) Ltd, Douglas House, Tollgate Park, Beaconside, Stafford, ST16 3EE

675   Stoke-on-Trent - Minehead

No vehicles are contracted to operate in National Express colours. The vehicles used on the service are selected from the main fleet. Details of the vehicles in this fleet may be found in The West Midlands Bus Handbook

LONDON COACHES

London Coaches (Kent) Ltd, Lower Road, Northfleet, DA11 9SN

010	London - Cambridge
024	London - Eastbourne
025	London - Brighton
035	London - Bournemouth
040	London - Bristol
570	London - Blackpool
650	London - Dover

No vehicles are contracted to operate in National Express colours and most carry North Kent Express fleet names. The vehicles used on the service are selected from the main fleet. Details of the vehicles in this fleet may be found in The South East Bus Handbook

MOORES

C Moore, 6 Hereford Way, Middlewich, CW10 9GS

538	Manchester Airport - Glasgow

No vehicles are contracted to operate in National Express colours. The vehicles used on the service are selected from the main fleet.

PARK'S

Parks of Hamilton (Coach Hirers) Ltd, 20 Bothwell Road, Hamilton, ML3 0AY

426	Glasgow - London
504	London - Truro
534	Glasgow - Hull
537	Glasgow - Lincoln
538	Glasgow - Manchester Airport
542	Glasgow - London
591	Edinburgh - London
595	Edinburgh - London

HSK651	Volvo B10M-62	Plaxton Paragon	C49FT	2000
HSK652	Volvo B10M-62	Plaxton Paragon	C49FT	2000
HSK653	Volvo B10M-62	Plaxton Paragon	C49FT	2000
HSK654	Volvo B10M-62	Plaxton Paragon	C49FT	2000

Details of the other coaches in this fleet may be found in The Scottish Bus Handbook

PIKES

J Pike, 77 Scott Close, Walworth Industrial Estate, Andover, SP10 5NU

532		Southampton - London			
	P181NAK	Dennis Javelin GX	Plaxton Premiere 350	C46FT	1997

Details of the vehicles in this fleet may be found in The West Midlands Bus Handbook

RAPSONS

Rapsons Coaches Ltd, 1 Seafield Road, Inverness, IV1 1TN

538		Coventry - Inverness				
588		London - Inverness				
590		Glasgow - London				
645	V943JST	Volvo B10M-62	Plaxton Première 350	C49FT	2000	
646	V944JST	Volvo B10M-62	Plaxton Première 350	C49FT	2000	
654	X465XAS	Volvo B10M-62	Plaxton Première 320	C49FT	2001	
658	TRM144	Volvo B10M-62	Plaxton Première 350	C48FT	1999	Wallace Arnold, 2001

Details of the vehicles in this fleet may be found in The Scottish Bus Handbook

The most northerly operator on the National Express network is Rapsons whose base is in Inverness although bus service operations extended north of mainland Scotland to the Orkneys and Shetland. Seen preparing for its next run south is 646, V944JST. *Phillip Stephenson*

ROWELLS

S Gardiner, 3B Dukesway, Low Prudhoe, NE42 6PQ

424	Newcastle - London

No vehicles are contracted to operate in National Express colours. The vehicles used on the service are selected from the main fleet. Details of the vehicles in this fleet may be found in The North East Bus Handbook

SELWYN'S

Selwyns Travel Ltd, Cavendish Farm Road, Weston, Runcorn, WA7 4LU

060	Liverpool - Manchester
303	Birkenhead - Southsea
327	Liverpool - Weymouth
383	Wrexham - Edinburgh
394	Middlesborough - Glasgow
420	London - Stafford
422	London - Burnley
440	London - Manchester
533	Wrexham - Glasgow
538	Manchester Airport - Glasgow
550	London – Birkenhead
550	London – Southport
551	London – Birkenhead
551	London – Liverpool
662	Liverpool - Skegness

Selwyns have been a regular performer on National Express for some years. Recent deliveries have been the latest versions of Van Hool-bodied DAF coaches. Now the oldest in the fleet is R39GNU, seen in Marlyebone while working route 420 from Stafford. *Gerry Mead*

From its base in Runcorn, Selwyns operate National Express routes both north and south. Expressliner II, R72ECA, is seen heading back to Wrexham on service 383 in Galashiels. *Tony Wilson*

39	M602BCA	Dennis Javelin GX 12SDA2161	Plaxton Premiére 350	C46FT	1995
62	Y467HUA	DAF DE33WSSB3000	Van Hool T9 Alizée	C49FT	2001
63	P522NMA	Volvo B10M-62	Plaxton Expressliner 2	C44FT	1996
64	Y468HUA	DAF DE33WSSB3000	Van Hool T9 Alizée	C49FT	2001
66	M366AMA	Dennis Javelin GX 12SDA2125	Plaxton Premiére 350	C46FT	1995
68	Y469HUA	DAF DE33WSSB3000	Van Hool T9 Alizée	C49FT	2001
69	R39GNW	DAF DE33WSSB3000	Van Hool Alizée HE	C49FT	1998
70	P70SEL	Volvo B10M-62	Plaxton Expressliner 2	C44FT	1996
71	R71ECA	Volvo B10M-62	Plaxton Expressliner 2	C44FT	1997
72	R72ECA	Volvo B10M-62	Plaxton Expressliner 2	C44FT	1997
73	R73KCA	Volvo B10M-62	Plaxton Expressliner 2	C44FT	1998
74	T174AUA	DAF DE33WSSB3000	Van Hool T9 Alizée	C44FT	1999
75	Y475HUA	DAF DE33WSSB3000	Van Hool T9 Alizée	C49FT	2001
76	Y476HUA	DAF DE33WSSB3000	Van Hool T9 Alizée	C49FT	2001
77	S428JUA	DAF DE33WSSB3000	Van Hool T9 Alizée	C49FT	1999
79	W226CDN	DAF DE33WSSB3000	Van Hool T9 Alizée	C49FT	2000
90	YJ51EKX	DAF DE33WSSB3000	Van Hool T9 Alizée	C49FT	2002
91	YJ51EKY	DAF DE33WSSB3000	Van Hool T9 Alizée	C49FT	2002
92	YJ51EKZ	DAF DE33WSSB3000	Van Hool T9 Alizée	C49FT	2002

Details of the other vehicles in this fleet may be found in The Cheshire & Merseyside Bus Handbook

SILVERDALE

Silverdale London Ltd, 3 Radford Estate, Old Oak Lane, London, NW10 6UA

420	London - Birmingham
540	London - Manchester

No vehicles are contracted to operate in National Express colours. The vehicles used on the service are selected from the main fleet.

STAGECOACH EAST

Cambus Ltd, 100 Cowley Road, Cambridge, CB4 4DN

010	London - Cambridge (to 11 August 2002)
448	London - Grimsby
448	London - Lincoln
448	London - Peterborough
449	London - Mablethorpe

445 - 456		Volvo B10M-62		Plaxton Expressliner 2		C49FT	1995-97		
445	N445XVA	**448**	N448XVA	**450**	N450XVA	**455**	R455FCE	**456**	R456FCE
446	N446XVA	**449**	N449XVA	**451**	N451XVA				

457	S457BCE	Volvo B10M-62	Jonckheere Mistral 50	C49FT	1988
458	S458BCE	Volvo B10M-62	Jonckheere Mistral 50	C49FT	1988
459	S459BCE	Volvo B10M-62	Jonckheere Mistral 50	C49FT	1988
460	S460BCE	Volvo B10M-62	Jonckheere Mistral 50	C49FT	1988

Details of the other vehicles in this fleet and other Stagecoach fleets may be found in the annual Stagecoach Bus Handbook

In recent years Stagecoach have chosen the Jonckheere Mistral 50 for their coaching needs and many are now used for their National Express contracts. Pictured in Pimlico is 457, S457BCE, from the Stagecoach East fleet. By the end of August 2002 Airlinks will have replaced Stagecoach on the 010 service to Cambridge.
Dave Heath

STAGECOACH EAST MIDLANDS

East Midland Motor Services Ltd, New Street, Chesterfield, Derbyshire, S40 2LQ

230	Gatwick Airport - Mansfield
230	Gatwick Airport - Nottingham
350	Liverpool - Cambridge
350	Liverpool - Sheffield

662	M808JTY	Volvo B10M-62	Plaxton Expressliner 2	C44FT	1995	Busways, 1997
663	R663TKU	Volvo B10M-62	Plaxton Expressliner 2	C44FT	1997	
664	R664TKU	Volvo B10M-62	Plaxton Expressliner 2	C44FT	1997	
665	S665SDT	Volvo B10M-62	Jonckheere Mistral 50	C44FT	1998	
668	T668XTV	Volvo B10M-62	Jonckheere Mistral 50	C44FT	1999	
669	T669XTV	Volvo B10M-62	Jonckheere Mistral 50	C44FT	1999	
674	S173SVK	Volvo B10M-62	Jonckheere Mistral 50	C44FT	1998	Stagecoach NE, 2001
675	S174SVK	Volvo B10M-62	Jonckheere Mistral 50	C44FT	1998	Stagecoach NE, 2001
676	KSU461	Volvo B10M-62	Jonckheere Mistral 50	C44FT	1999	Stagecoach NE, 2001
677	KSU462	Volvo B10M-62	Jonckheere Mistral 50	C44FT	1999	Stagecoach NE, 2001

Details of the other vehicles in this fleet and other Stagecoach fleets may be found in the annual Stagecoach Bus Handbook

The Jonckheere Mistral is the higher version of the current coach range from this Belgian manufacturer and five from this fleet carry *Flightlink* **colours for Gatwick airport services. One of the pair now based at Mansfield is 668, T668XTV, seen working route 350 in Manchester.** *Mark Doggett*

STAGECOACH NORTH WEST

Stagecoach (North West) Ltd
2/F Broadacre House, 16-20 Lowther Street, Carlisle, CA3 8DA

023	London - Bexhill
325	Manchester - Birmingham
333	Blackpool - Bournemouth
341	Burnley - Paignton
540	London - Burnley
540	London - Bury
540	London - Colne
540	London - Manchester
570	London - Blackpool
570	London - Whitehaven
590	London - Aberdeen

130	N130VAO	Volvo B10M-62	Plaxton Expressliner 2	C46FT	1995	
131	N131VAO	Volvo B10M-62	Plaxton Expressliner 2	C46FT	1995	
132	N132VAO	Volvo B10M-62	Plaxton Expressliner 2	C46FT	1995	
133	S133KRM	Volvo B10M-62	Jonckheere Mistral 50	C44FT	1998	
134	S134KRM	Volvo B10M-62	Jonckheere Mistral 50	C44FT	1998	
8120	R120VFR	Volvo B10M-62	Jonckheere Mistral 50	C44FT	1998	
1121	S905JHG	Volvo B10M-62	Jonckheere Mistral 50	C44FT	1998	
1122	L126NAO	Volvo B10M-62	Plaxton Expressliner 2	C46FT	1994	Stagecoach Cumberland, 1999
1124	M406BFG	Volvo B10M-62	Plaxton Premiére 350	C51FT	1995	Stagecoach Bluebird, 2000
1125	L125NAO	Volvo B10M-62	Plaxton Expressliner 2	C46FT	1994	Stagecoach Cumberland, 1998
1126	S906JHG	Volvo B10M-62	Jonckheere Mistral 50	C44FT	1998	
1128	N128VAO	Volvo B10M-62	Plaxton Expressliner 2	C44FT	1994	Stagecoach Cumberland, 2000
1129	N129NAO	Volvo B10M-62	Plaxton Expressliner 2	C44FT	1994	Stagecoach Cumberland, 2000
8131	N447XVA	Volvo B10M-62	Plaxton Expressliner 2	C49FT	1995	Stagecoach East, 2001
1164	M164SCK	Volvo B10M-62	Plaxton Expressliner 2	C46FT	1994	
1165	M165SCK	Volvo B10M-62	Plaxton Expressliner 2	C46FT	1994	

Details of the other vehicles in this fleet and other Stagecoach fleets may be found in the annual Stagecoach Bus Handbook

Stagecoach's National Express coaches are all based on the Volvo B10M chassis. The North West fleet is based on Carlisle and supplies the operations of Ribble and Cumberland. Pictured in Marylebone is Jonckheere Mistral 8120, R120VFR. Currently two of the Expressliners are in Flightlink colours. *Gerry Mead*

STAGECOACH SCOTLAND

Bluebird Buses Ltd, Guild Street, Aberdeen, AB9 2DR

535		Kettering - Dundee				
596		London - Glenrothes				
621	T667XTV	Volvo B10M-62	Jonckheere Mistral 50	C44FT	1999	Stagecoach East Midland, 2000
622	P622ESO	Volvo B10M-62	Plaxton Expressliner 2	C44FT	1997	
625	P625NSE	Volvo B10M-62	Plaxton Expressliner 2	C44FT	1997	
626	P626NSE	Volvo B10M-62	Plaxton Expressliner 2	C44FT	1997	
627	P627ESO	Volvo B10M-62	Plaxton Expressliner 2	C44FT	1997	

Details of the other vehicles in this fleet and other Stagecoach fleets may be found in the annual Stagecoach Bus Handbook

Until recently Stagecoach Western Buses operate two vehicles on the euroLines service from London to Belfast that passes through Stranraer though these have now been replaced by a further pair from Ulsterbus. Pictured in Bluewater is Stagecoach South East's 8914, M914WJK. This is one of the coaches due for replacement by the third generation of Expressliners, this time based on the Plaxton Paragon. *Colin Lloyd*

STAGECOACH SOUTH EAST

Stagecoach East Kent Ltd, Bus Station, St George's Lane, Canterbury, CT1 2SY

020	London - Dover	
021	London - Dover	
022	London - Ramsgate	
024	London - Hastings	

8405	M405BFG	Volvo B10M-62	Plaxton Premiére 350	C53F	1995
8410	XSU612	Volvo B10M-62	Plaxton Premiére 350	C51FT	1995
8901	S901CCD	Volvo B10M-62	Jonckheere Mistral 50	C49FT	1998
8902	S902CCD	Volvo B10M-62	Jonckheere Mistral 50	C49FT	1998
8903	S903CCD	Volvo B10M-62	Jonckheere Mistral 50	C49FT	1998

8904 - 8909   Volvo B10M-62   Jonckheere Mistral 50   C49FT   1999

8904	V904DPN	8906	V906DPN	8907	V907DDY	8908	V908DDY	8909	V909DDY
8905	V905DPN								

8913 - 8918   Volvo B10M-62   Plaxton Expressliner 2   C49FT   1994-95

8913	M913WJK	8915	M915WJK	8916	M916WJK	8917	M917WJK	8918	M918WJK
8914	M914WJK								

Details of the other vehicles in this fleet and other Stagecoach fleets may be found in the annual Stagecoach Bus Handbook

Coaches allocated to the frequent 020 route from Dover to London carry *Shuttle* markings. Pictured at the Elephant & Castle is Mistral 8907, V907DDY from the Dover depot where the National Express coaching unit is located. Ten Volvo B12M coaches with Plaxton Paragon Expressliner bodywork are expected to displace the earlier Expressliners later in 2002. *Gerry Mead*

STAGECOACH SOUTH MIDLANDS

Midland Red (South) Ltd, Railway Terrace, Rugby, Warwickshire, CV21 3HS

310	Bradford - Leicester
320	Birmingham - Bradford
320	Oxford - Bradford
324	Paignton - Bradford
337	Brixham - Rugby
455	London - Northampton
455	London - Rugby
460	London - Stratford-upon-Avon
460	London - Coventry
561	London - Bradford

30	N618USS	Volvo B10M-62	Plaxton Expressliner 2	C44FT	1995	Stagecoach Bluebird, 2000
31	N452XVA	Volvo B10M-62	Plaxton Expressliner 2	C49FT	1997	Stagecoach Cambus, 2000
32	R453FCE	Volvo B10M-62	Plaxton Expressliner 2	C49FT	1997	Stagecoach Cambus, 2000
33	R454FCE	Volvo B10M-62	Plaxton Expressliner 2	C49FT	1997	Stagecoach Cambus (V), 2000

34 - 39		Volvo B10M-62	Plaxton Expressliner 2	C46FT	1997	
34	R34AKV	**36**	R36AKV	**37**	R37AKV	**38**	R38AKV	**39**	R39AKV
35	R35AKV								

61	T661OBD	Volvo B10M-62	Jonckheere Mistral 50	C44FT	1999
62	T662OBD	Volvo B10M-62	Jonckheere Mistral 50	C44FT	1999
63	T663OBD	Volvo B10M-62	Jonckheere Mistral 50	C44FT	1999

Details of the other vehicles in this fleet and other Stagecoach fleets may be found in the annual Stagecoach Bus Handbook

Three coaches were delivered to Stagecoach South Midlands in 1999 for National Express work. Pictured in Chesterfield while working route 320 is number 662, T662OBD. *Tony Wilson*

STAGECOACH WEST & WALES

Cheltenham & Gloucester Omnibus Company Ltd
3/4 Bath Street, Cheltenham, GL50 1YE

| 412 | London - Worcester |
| 412 | London - Gloucester |

550	R550JDF	Volvo B10M-62	Plaxton Expressliner 2	C48FT	1997	
551	R551JDF	Volvo B10M-62	Plaxton Expressliner 2	C48FT	1997	
552	R552JDF	Volvo B10M-62	Plaxton Expressliner 2	C48FT	1997	
553	R553JDF	Volvo B10M-62	Plaxton Expressliner 2	C48FT	1997	
554	R554JDF	Volvo B10M-62	Plaxton Expressliner 2	C48FT	1997	
562	P92URG	Volvo B10M-62	Plaxton Expressliner 2	C47FT	1996	Stagecoach NE, 2001

Details of the other vehicles in this fleet and other Stagecoach fleets may be found in the annual Stagecoach Bus Handbook

STEPHENSONS

D Stephenson, Stillington Road, Easingwold, York, YO61 3DZ

| 561 | London - Bradford |

No vehicles are contracted to operate in National Express colours. The vehicles used on the service are selected from the main fleet. Details of the other vehicles in this fleet may be found in the Yorkshire Bus Handbook

Stagecoach West & Wales' undertake their National Express work from the Cheltenham garage. The fleet was augmented in 2001 with the arrival of two further coaches with 562, P92URG seen heading east on their only route, the 412. *Dave Heath*

TELLINGS GOLDEN MILLER

Tellings Golden Miller, 20A Wintersells Road, Byfleet, West Byfleet, KT14 7LF

030	Portsmouth - London
032	Portsmouth - London
032	Southampton - London
300	Southsea - Bristol
310	Southsea - Bradford

N20TGM	Volvo B10M-62	Van Hool Alizèe HE	C48FT	1996
R10TGM	Volvo B10M-62	Van Hool T9 Alizèe	C48FT	1998
R20TGM	Volvo B10M-62	Van Hool T9 Alizèe	C48FT	1998
KP51SYF	Volvo B10M-62	Plaxton Panther	C49FT	2002
KP51UEV	Volvo B10M-62	Plaxton Panther	C49FT	2002
KP51UEW	Volvo B10M-62	Plaxton Panther	C49FT	2002
KP51UEX	Volvo B10M-62	Plaxton Panther	C49FT	2002
KP51UEY	Volvo B10M-62	Plaxton Panther	C49FT	2002
KP51UEZ	Volvo B10M-62	Plaxton Panther	C49FT	2002
KU02YUF	Volvo B12M	Plaxton Paragon	C49FT	2002
KU02YUG	Volvo B12M	Plaxton Paragon	C49FT	2002

Details of the other vehicles in this fleet may be found in the South East Bus Handbook

Recently delivered to Tellings Golden Miller are a further pair of Plaxton Paragon Expressliners. Pictured heading for Southsea, KU02YUG illustrates the near side styling of the model as it pulls out of Chesterfield bus station. *Mark Doggett*

T M TRAVEL

J M & T J Watts, Fan Road, Staveley, S43 3PT

690	Derby - Scarborough

No vehicles are contracted to operate in National Express colours. The vehicles used on the service are selected from the main fleet. The vehicles used on the service are selected from the main fleet. Details of the vehicles in this fleet may be found in the East Midlands Bus Handbook

TIM'S TRAVEL

Tim's Travel Ltd, The Coach Station, Dorset Road, Sheerness, Kent, ME12 1LT

020	London - Dover

No vehicles are contracted to operate in National Express colours. The vehicles used on the service are selected from the main fleet. Details of the vehicles in this fleet may be found in The South East Bus Handbook

TM Travel operate the Saturday service to Scarborough. Though they have this one return journey each week, Expressliner II K387DWN retains National Express colours. It is seen on other duties during the week.
Tony Wilson

TRATHENS

Trathens Travel Services Ltd, Walkham Park, Burrington Way, Plymouth, PL5 3LS

421	London - Blackpool
500	London - Penzance
501	London - Plymouth
504	London - Penzance
538	Manchester Airport - Aberdeen
540	London - Rochdale/Bolton
570	London - Blackpool - Fleetwood
592	London - Aberdeen

	P926KYC	Volvo B12T	Van Hool Astrobel	C57/14CT	1997
	P927KYC	Volvo B12T	Van Hool Astrobel	C57/14CT	1997
	R261OFJ	Volvo B12T	Van Hool Astrobel	C57/14CT	1998
500	LSK500	Volvo B10M-62	Jonckheere Mistral 50	C49FT	2001
501	LSK501	Volvo B10M-62	Jonckheere Mistral 50	C49FT	2001
502	LSK502	Volvo B10M-62	Jonckheere Mistral 50	C49FT	2001
503	LSK503	Volvo B10M-62	Jonckheere Mistral 50	C49FT	2001
504	LSK504	Volvo B10M-62	Jonckheere Mistral 50	C49FT	2001
505	LSK505	Volvo B10M-62	Jonckheere Mistral 50	C49FT	2001
506	LSK506	Volvo B10M-62	Jonckheere Mistral 50	C49FT	2001
507	LSK507	Volvo B10M-62	Jonckheere Mistral 50	C49FT	2001
508	LSK508	Volvo B10M-62	Jonckheere Mistral 50	C49FT	2001
511	YN51XMU	Neoplan N122/3	Neoplan Skyliner	C57/14FT	2001
512	YN51XMV	Neoplan N122/3	Neoplan Skyliner	C57/14FT	2001
513	YN51XMW	Neoplan N122/3	Neoplan Skyliner	C57/14FT	2001
514	YN51XMX	Neoplan N122/3	Neoplan Skyliner	C57/14FT	2001
515	YN51XMK	Neoplan N122/3	Neoplan Skyliner	C57/14FT	2001
516	YN51XML	Neoplan N122/3	Neoplan Skyliner	C57/14FT	2001
517	YN51XMZ	Neoplan N122/3	Neoplan Skyliner	C57/14FT	2001
518	YN51XNC	Neoplan N122/3	Neoplan Skyliner	C57/14FT	2001
519	YN51XND	Neoplan N122/3	Neoplan Skyliner	C57/14FT	2001
520	YN51XNE	Neoplan N122/3	Neoplan Skyliner	C57/14FT	2001
521	YN51XMH	Neoplan N122/3	Neoplan Skyliner	C57/14FT	2001
522	YN51XMJ	Neoplan N122/3	Neoplan Skyliner	C57/14FT	2001

Details of the vehicles in this fleet may be found in The South West Bus Handbook

TRENT

Trent Motor Traction Co Ltd, 88A Mansfield Road, Heanor, Derbyshire, DE75 7BG

326	Nottingham - Newcastle
440	London - Derby
450	London - Mansfield
450	London - Retford

9	V209JAL	Volvo B10M-62	Plaxton Expressliner 2	C49FT	1999
10	V210JAL	Volvo B10M-62	Plaxton Expressliner 2	C49FT	1999
11	V211JAL	Volvo B10M-62	Plaxton Expressliner 2	C49FT	1999
12	V212JAL	Volvo B10M-62	Plaxton Expressliner 2	C49FT	1999
13	X913ERA	Volvo B10M-62	Plaxton Expressliner 2	C49FT	2000
14	X914ERA	Volvo B10M-62	Plaxton Expressliner 2	C49FT	2000
15	X915ERA	Volvo B10M-62	Plaxton Expressliner 2	C49FT	2000

Details of the other vehicles in this fleet may be found in The East Midland Bus Handbook

Passing through Golders Green while making its way towards the M1 motorway, YN51XML is one of the new generation of double-deck coaches for National Express work which have displaced Van Hool Astrobel models. So far twelve Neoplan Skyiners have arrived with Trathens now the only authorised operators of double-decks which supply an extensive network from their base in Plymouth. *Dave Heath*

Trent's seven identical coaches for their National Express duties are based at Derby. Seen in Wetherby is number 10, V210JAL. As a result of customer surveys, which indicated that customers were preferring to bring their own individual refreshments, we stopped all on-board catering on National Express services on 2nd April 2001. This means that the name *RAPIDE* branding has been dropped from the vehicles. Refreshment services are still retained on Flightlink services as an added benefit to this higher value product. *Tony Wilson*

TRURONIAN

Truronian Ltd, 24 Lemon Street, Truro, Cornwall, TR1 2LS

314	Brighton – Perranporth
329	Newquay - Leeds
329	Newquay - Manchester
505	Newquay - London

No vehicles are contracted to operate in National Express colours. The vehicles used on the service are selected from the main fleet. Details of the vehicles in this fleet may be found in The South West Bus Handbook

TURNER'S

Turners Coachways (Bristol) Ltd, 59 Days Road, St Phillips, Bristol, BS2 0QS

040	London - Bristol

No vehicles are contracted to operate in National Express colours. The vehicles used on the service are selected from the main fleet. Details of the vehicles in this fleet may be found in The South West Bus Handbook

ULSTERBUS

Ulsterbus Ltd, Milewater Road, Belfast, BT3 9BG

euroLines services to Eire, including those from Birmingham to Waterford.

691	ACZ6691	Volvo B10M-62	Plaxton Excalibur	C49FT	1999
692	ACZ6692	Volvo B10M-62	Plaxton Excalibur	C49FT	1999
1659	BCZ1659	Volvo B10M-62	Plaxton Excalibur	C49FT	1999
1660	BCZ1660	Volvo B10M-62	Plaxton Excalibur	C49FT	1999

No vehicles are contracted to operate in National Express colours. The vehicles used on the service are selected from the main fleet. Details of the vehicles in this fleet may be found in The Ireland & Islands Bus Handbook

VOEL COACHES

Voel Coaches, Dyserth, Rhyl, Denbighshire, LL18 6BP

662	Liverpool - Skegness

No vehicles are contracted to operate in National Express colours. The vehicles used on the service are selected from the main fleet. Details of the vehicles in this fleet may be found in The Welsh Bus Handbook

WILTS & DORSET

Wilts & Dorset Bus Co Ltd, Towngate House, 2-8 Parkstone Road, Poole, BH15 2PR

| 032 | London - Salisbury |
| 033 | London - Yeovil |

3216	T216REL	DAF DE33WSSB3000	Plaxton Prima	C49FT	1999
3217	T217REL	DAF DE33WSSB3000	Plaxton Prima	C49FT	1999
3218	T218REL	DAF DE33WSSB3000	Plaxton Prima	C49FT	1999

Details of the other vehicles in this fleet may be found in The South West Bus Handbook

WISDOM

T O Wisdom, 58 Reginald Street, Leeds, LS7 3HL

561   Bradford - London

No vehicles are contracted to operate in National Express colours. The vehicles used on the service are selected from the main fleet.

Ulsterbus provide two coaches for the euroLines services from Northern Ireland. These are Volvo B10Ms with Plaxton Excalibur bodywork. Pictured arriving in Edinburgh is 1659, BCZ1659. *Brian Ridgway*

YARDLEY'S

Yardley's Travel Ltd, 68-72 Berkeley Road East, Hay Mills, Birmingham, B25 8NP

310	Coventry - Leeds
310	Birmingham - Leeds
661	Birmingham - Skegness
694	Birmingham - Llandudno

No vehicles are contracted to operate in National Express colours. The vehicles used on the service are selected from the main fleet.

YEOMANS

Yeomans Canyon Travel Ltd, 21-3 Three Elms Trading Estate, Hereford, HR4 9PU

| 412 | Hereford - London |
| 413 | Hereford - London |

56	M342SCJ	Volvo B10M-62	Plaxton Expressliner 2	C44FT	1995
57	M343SCJ	Volvo B10M-62	Plaxton Expressliner 2	C44FT	1995
64	W634MKY	Volvo B10M-62	Plaxton Expressliner 2	C44FT	2000

Yorkshire Traction added a pair or Plaxton Paragon Expressliners in 2001 on Volvo B10M chassis with a further pair on its successor, the B12M in 2002. Seen en route for London in 66, Y966PHL. *Tony Wilson*

YORKSHIRE TRACTION

The Yorkshire Traction Co Ltd, Upper Sheffield Road, Barnsley, S70 4PP

070	Sheffield - Leeds
070	Sheffield - Bradford
310	Bradford - Poole
312	Barnsley - Blackpool
335	Halifax - Poole
351	Blackpool - Sheffield
406	London - Newquay
465	London - Huddersfield
502	London - Ilfracombe
560	London - Barnsley
560	London - Rotherham
561	London - Leeds
564	London - Halifax

42	6078HE	DAF DE33WSSB3000	Van Hool Alizée H	C44FT	1998	Arriva Yorkshire, 2000
45	V345EKW	Mercedes-Benz O404-15R	Hispano Vita	C44FT	2000	
47	T870RGA	Volvo B10M-62	Plaxton Première 350	C49FT	1999	Parks of Hamilton, 2001
48	T871RGA	Volvo B10M-62	Plaxton Première 350	C49FT	1999	Parks of Hamilton, 2001
49	T872RGA	Volvo B10M-62	Plaxton Première 350	C49FT	1999	Parks of Hamilton, 2001
53	HE5362	Volvo B10M-60	Plaxton Première 350	C46FT	1993	
54	RHE194	Volvo B10M-60	Plaxton Première 350	C46FT	1993	
55	HE8054	Volvo B10M-62	Plaxton Première 350	C46FT	1995	
56	2316HE	Volvo B10M-62	Plaxton Première 350	C46FT	1995	
57	YTC838	Volvo B10M-62	Plaxton Première 350	C46FT	1995	
58	6341HE	Volvo B10M-62	Plaxton Première 350	C44FT	1997	
59	5562HE	Volvo B10M-62	Plaxton Première 350	C44FT	1997	
60	3030HE	Volvo B10M-62	Plaxton Première 350	C44FT	1997	

Yorkshire Traction took the development Mercedes-Benz coach for National Express duties in 2000. This model O404 number is numbered 45, V345EKW, and carries a Hispano Vita body that meets National Express criteria. The main routes operated by 'Tracky' are London routes from Yorkshire and Trans-Pennine journeys to Blackpool, a destination served since the end of the Second World War. *Dave Heath*

61	6087HE	Volvo B10M-62	Plaxton Expressliner 2	C44FT	1998	
62	R762XWG	Volvo B10M-62	Plaxton Expressliner 2	C44FT	1998	
63	R763XWG	Volvo B10M-62	Plaxton Expressliner 2	C44FT	1998	
64	S364VKW	Volvo B10M-62	Plaxton Expressliner 2	C44FT	1999	
65	S365VKW	Volvo B10M-62	Plaxton Expressliner 2	C44FT	1999	
66	Y966PHL	Volvo B10M-62	Plaxton Paragon	C49FT	2001	
67	Y967PHL	Volvo B10M-62	Plaxton Paragon	C49FT	2001	
68	YS02YXR	Volvo B12M	Plaxton Paragon	C49FT	2002	
69	YS02YXT	Volvo B12M	Plaxton Paragon	C49FT	2002	
71	2542HE	Scania K93CRB	Plaxton Paramount 3500 III	C46FT	1991	to be withdrawn 2002
75	OHE50	Scania K93CRB	Plaxton Paramount 3500 III	C46FT	1991	to be withdrawn 2002
81	4195HE	Scania K113CRB	Van Hool Alizée HE	C46FT	1996	
82	1533HE	Scania K113CRB	Van Hool Alizée HE	C46FT	1996	

Previous Registrations:

1533HE	N282CAK	4195HE	N281CAK	OHE50	J694YWJ
2316HE	M656VWE	6087HE	R761XWG	RHE194	L54NWJ
2542HE	J293YHE	HE5362	L53NWJ	YTC838	M957VKY
3030HE	K803FWE	HE8054	M655VWE		

Details of the other vehicles in this fleet may be found in The Yorkshire Bus Handbook

ZAK'S

K P Fazakarkey, 319 Shady Lane, Great Barr, Birmingham, B44 9XA

329	Birmingham - Newquay
420	Shrewsbury - London
460	Coventry - London

No vehicles are contracted to operate in National Express colours. The vehicles used on the service are selected from the main fleet. Details of the vehicles in this fleet may be found in The West Midlands Bus Handbook

Buckingham Palace Road is the location for this view of Selwyn's 90, YJ51EKX taken at the start of the Summer schedule. Its arrival brought the number of the new Van Hool Alizee's operated in National Express colours by the company to eleven. *Colin Lloyd*

Index to National Express routes

euroLines Services from England

120-4/6	London - Amiens - Paris	170-4	London - Eindhoven - northern Germany
121/221	London - Disneyland - Paris	180/1	London - Madrid - Seville - Algeciras
121/3	London - Paris - Portugal	182	London - Madrid
125	Amsterdam - Brussels - Paris	183/5	London - Bordeaux - Lourdes
127/8	London - Bilbao - Oviedo		- San Sebastian - Zaragoza
129	London - La Coruna	184/6/9	London - Toulouse - Andorra
130-3	London - Geneva	187	London - Nantes - La Rochelle
130/1	London - Clermont Ferrand	188	London - Arcahon - Bayonne
131/2	London - Lyon - Chamonix	190/1/6	London - Salzburg - Vienna
132/4	London - Marseille - Nice	190	London - Bratislava - Kosice
132/5	London - Avignon - Narbonne	191	London - Vienna - Budapest
137	London - Strasbourg - Zurich	192	London - Prague - Ostrava
140-4	London - Amsterdam	193	London - Warsaw
168	London - Arnhem	194	London - Krakow
142(274)	London - Amsterdam - Berlin	195	London - Olsztyn
140(274)	London - Amsterdam - Hamburg	162(498)	London - Frankfurt - Belgrade
146	London - Copenhagen	162(418)	London - Frankfurt - Sarajevo
147	London - Alborg/Hirtshals	163(497)	London - Zagreb
151	London - Milan - Rome	163(409)	London - Split
152-5	London - Genoa - Sienna - Venice	163(250)	London - Frankfurt - Bucharest
160/1	London - Barcelona - Murcia	284/5	London - Sweden
162/3/5	London - Frankfurt - Munich	876	Holyhead - Birmingham - Brussels
164	London - Cologne - Dresden		- Frankfurt - Munich
167/8	London - Lille - Brussels		
169	London - Brussels - Luxembourg		

During 1993 one of the first major acquisitions by the group was the Amsterdam based company, euroLines Nederland BV, which helped to strengthen the growing euroLines network of European coach services. Seen in livery is KMP's N77KMP. As we go to press a further pair of Neoplan coaches has entered service bringing the number of this type to three. Across Europe a wide variety of coach models are used many originating from their host countries. *Colin Lloyd*

Vehicle Index

Reg	Operator	Reg	Operator	Reg	Operator	Reg	Operator
240FRH	Ambassador	M110PWN	First - Cymru	N913KHW	First – Somerset	R351LPR	Bournemouth
662NKR	Arriva Fox	M111PWN	First - Cymru	N914KHW	First – Somerset	R354NRU	Bournemouth
865GAT	First - Avon	M122UUB	Arriva North East	NK51ORJ	Durham Travel	R355NRU	Bournemouth
1533HE	Yorkshire Traction	M131HJR	Durham Travel	NK51ORL	Durham Travel	R453FCE	Stagecoach South Mid
2316HE	Yorkshire Traction	M164SCK	Stagecoach NW	NK51ORN	Durham Travel	R454FCE	Stagecoach South Mid
2542HE	Yorkshire Traction	M165SCK	Stagecoach NW	NK51ORO	Durham Travel	R455FCE	Stagecoach East
3030HE	Yorkshire Traction	M301BRL	First – Devon & C	OHE50	Yorkshire Traction	R456FCE	Stagecoach East
4195HE	Yorkshire Traction	M302BRL	First – Devon & C	P24	Durham Travel	R550JDF	Stagecoach West
5562HE	Yorkshire Traction	M303BRL	First – Devon & C	P31XUG	Arriva Yorkshire	R551JDF	Stagecoach West
6078HE	Yorkshire Traction	M342SCJ	Yeomans	P56XNL	Durham Travel	R552JDF	Stagecoach West
6341HE	Yorkshire Traction	M343SCJ	Yeomans	P57XNL	Durham Travel	R553JDF	Stagecoach West
A1YBG	Arriva Yorkshire	M366AMA	Selwyns	P70SEL	Selwyns	R554JDF	Stagecoach West
A2YBG	Arriva Yorkshire	M405BFG	Stagecoach SE	P92URG	Stagecoach West	R663TKU	Stagecoach East Mid
A4YBG	Arriva Yorkshire	M406BFG	Stagecoach SE	P201RWR	Arriva Fox	R664TKU	Stagecoach East Mid
A7XCL	Excelsior	M440FHW	First – Somerset	P205RWR	Arriva Fox	R761XWG	Yorkshire Traction
A8XCL	Excelsior	M441BDM	Birmingham Coach	P234BFJ	First – Devon & C	R762XWG	Yorkshire Traction
A9FTG	Dunn-Line	M602BCA	Selwyns	P235CTA	First – Devon & C	R763XWG	Yorkshire Traction
A9XCL	Excelsior	M743KJU	Ambassador	P236CTA	First – Devon & C	R813HWS	First – Somerset
BCZ1659	Ulsterbus	M765CWS	First – Somerset	P251AUT	Express Travel	R814HWS	First – Somerset
BCZ1660	Ulsterbus	M808JTY	Stagecoach East Mid	P352ARU	Bournemouth	R943LHT	First – Somerset
CN51XNU	Bebb Travel	M913WJK	Stagecoach SE	P353ARU	Bournemouth	RHE194	Yorkshire Traction
CN51XNV	Bebb Travel	M914WJK	Stagecoach SE	P411MDT	Ambassador	RYG684	Chenery
CN51XNW	Bebb Travel	M915WJK	Stagecoach SE	P412MDT	Ambassador	S26DTS	Durham Travel
CN51XNX	Bebb Travel	M916WJK	Stagecoach SE	P521PRL	First – Devon & C	S27DTS	Durham Travel
CN51XNY	Bebb Travel	M917WJK	Stagecoach SE	P522NMA	Selwyns	S116RKG	First - Cymru
CN51XNZ	Bebb Travel	M918WJK	Stagecoach SE	P522PRL	First – Devon & C	S133KRM	Stagecoach NW
CU6860	Go-Northern	M92BOU	First – Somerset	P622ESO	Stagecoach Scotland	S134KRM	Stagecoach NW
CU7661	Go-Northern	N20TGM	Tellings Golden Miller	P625NSE	Stagecoach Scotland	S173SVK	Stagecoach East Mid
FCU190	Go-Northern	N21ARC	Airlinks	P626NSE	Stagecoach Scotland	S174SVK	Stagecoach East Mid
GSK962	Go-Northern	N22DTS	Durham Travel	P627ESO	Stagecoach Scotland	S295WOA	Dunn-Line
HE5362	Yorkshire Traction	N23RTN	Durham Travel	P803BLJ	Ambassador	S296WOA	Dunn-Line
HE8054	Yorkshire Traction	N40SLK	Airlinks	P804BLJ	First - Cymru	S297WOA	Dunn-Line
HSK651	Parks of Hamilton	N50SLK	Airlinks	P837XAG	East Yorkshire	S298WOA	Dunn-Line
HSK652	Parks of Hamilton	N60SLK	Airlinks	P842WUG	Express Travel	S311SCV	First – Devon & C
HSK653	Parks of Hamilton	N70SLK	Airlinks	P926KYC	Trathens	S312SCV	First – Devon & C
HSK654	Parks of Hamilton	N80SLK	Airlinks	P927KYC	Trathens	S313SCV	First – Devon & C
JCN822	Go-Northern	N90SLK	Airlinks	P944RWS	First – Somerset	S314SRL	First – Devon & C
KP51SYF	Tellings Golden Miller	N112EWJ	First - Cymru	P945RWS	First – Somerset	S315SRL	First – Devon & C
KP51UEV	Tellings Golden Miller	N113VWN	First - Cymru	P946RWS	First – Somerset	S364OOB	Dunn-Line
KP51UEW	Tellings Golden Miller	N114VWN	First - Cymru	R20TGM	Tellings Golden Miller	S364VKW	Yorkshire Traction
KP51UEX	Tellings Golden Miller	N115VWN	First - Cymru	R34AKV	Stagecoach South Mid	S365OOB	Dunn-Line
KP51UEY	Tellings Golden Miller	N128VAO	Stagecoach NW	R35AKV	Stagecoach South Mid	S365VKW	Yorkshire Traction
KP51UEZ	Tellings Golden Miller	N129NAO	Stagecoach NW	R36AKV	Stagecoach South Mid	S428JUA	Selwyns
KSU461	Stagecoach East Mid	N130VAO	Stagecoach NW	R37AKV	Stagecoach South Mid	S457BCE	Stagecoach East
KSU462	Stagecoach East Mid	N131VAO	Stagecoach NW	R38AKV	Stagecoach South Mid	S458BCE	Stagecoach East
KU02YUF	Tellings Golden Miller	N132VAO	Stagecoach NW	R39AKV	Stagecoach South Mid	S459BCE	Stagecoach East
KU02YUG	Tellings Golden Miller	N170AAG	Birmingham Coach	R39AWO	Chenery	S460BCE	Stagecoach East
L28ABB	Durham Travel	N171AAG	Birmingham Coach	R39GNW	Selwyns	S665SDT	Stagecoach East Mid
L125NAO	Stagecoach NW	N172AAG	Birmingham Coach	R71ECA	Selwyns	S809DUR	Excelsior
L126NAO	Stagecoach NW	N173AAG	Birmingham Coach	R72ECA	Selwyns	S901CCD	Stagecoach SE
L506GEP	First - Cymru	N212TBC	Arriva Fox	R73KCA	Selwyns	S902CCD	Stagecoach SE
L705PHE	Express Travel	N232WFJ	First – Devon & C	R85DVF	Ambassador	S903CCD	Stagecoach SE
L707PHE	Express Travel	N233WFJ	First – Devon & C	R10TGM	Tellings Golden Miller	S905JHG	Stagecoach NW
L708PHE	Express Travel	N319NHY	First – Somerset	R120VFR	Stagecoach NW	S906JHG	Stagecoach NW
L709PHE	Express Travel	N320NHY	First – Somerset	R161GNW	Galloway	S930ATO	Airlinks
L710PHE	Express Travel	N321NHY	First – Somerset	R175VWN	First - Cymru	S977ABR	Go-Northern
L711PHE	Express Travel	N322NHY	First – Somerset	R176VWN	First - Cymru	S978ABR	Go-Northern
L712PHE	Express Travel	N369TJT	Birmingham Coach	R177VWN	First - Cymru	S979ABR	Go-Northern
L713PHE	Express Travel	N370TJT	Birmingham Coach	R178VWN	First - Cymru	T36EUA	Arriva Yorkshire
L714PHE	Express Travel	N445XVA	Stagecoach East	R256FBJ	Galloway	T37EUA	Arriva Yorkshire
LSK500	Trathens	N446XVA	Stagecoach East	R261OFJ	Trathens	T38EUA	Arriva Yorkshire
LSK501	Trathens	N447XVA	Stagecoach NW	R297AYB	First - Avon	T101XDE	First - Cymru
LSK502	Trathens	N448XVA	Stagecoach East	R297AYB	First – Devon & C	T102XDE	First - Cymru
LSK503	Trathens	N449XVA	Stagecoach East	R299AYB	First - Avon	T103XDE	First - Cymru
LSK504	Trathens	N450XVA	Stagecoach East	R303EEX	Chenery	T119AUA	Arriva Fox
LSK505	Trathens	N451XVA	Stagecoach East	R304EEX	Chenery	T174AUA	Selwyns
LSK506	Trathens	N452XVA	Stagecoach South Mid	R304JAF	First – Devon & C	T209XVO	Arriva Fox
LSK507	Trathens	N471KHU	First – Somerset	R305JAF	First – Devon & C	T216REL	Wilts & Dorset
LSK508	Trathens	N472KHU	First – Somerset	R307JAF	First – Devon & C	T217REL	Wilts & Dorset
M35KAX	Ambassador	N473KHU	First – Somerset	R308JAF	First – Devon & C 8	T218REL	Wilts & Dorset
M37HJR	Durham Travel	N474KHU	First – Somerset	R309JAF	First – Devon & C	T310AHY	First – Somerset
M38HJR	Durham Travel	N616USS	Stagecoach Scotland	R310JAF	First – Devon & C	T316KCV	First – Devon & C
M39HJR	Durham Travel	N617USS	Stagecoach Scotland	R326NRU	Bournemouth	T330AFX	Bournemouth
M41FTC	First – Somerset	N618USS	Stagecoach South Mid	R327NRU	Bournemouth	T331AFX	Bournemouth
M67AAG	Birmingham Coach	N821KWS	First – Somerset	R329NRU	Bournemouth	T661OBD	Stagecoach SM
M109PWN	First - Cymru	N822KWS	First – Somerset	R350LPR	Bournemouth		

These 'Pool' networks greatly increased travel opportunities for the rapidly growing number of coach passengers. Two of the most famous coaching 'Pools' were Associated Motorways, based at Cheltenham, and London Coastal Coaches, based at the new Victoria Coach Station. Opened in 1932, the new coach station replaced the original 'London' terminus in Lupus Street, which had opened in 1924. The Victoria site remains that of the London termin, though frequently refurbished since 1932s. Yorkshire Traction's Y966PHL is seen in Buckingham Palace Road, London in 2002. *Colin Lloyd*

T662OBD	Stagecoach SM	V906DPN	Stagecoach SE	X20NAT	Bruce's	Y783MFT	Go-Northern
T663OBD	Stagecoach SM	V907DDY	Stagecoach SE	X46CNY	Bebb Travel	Y784MFT	Go-Northern
T667XTV	Stagecoach Scotland	V908DDY	Stagecoach SE	X47CNY	Bebb Travel	Y785MFT	Go-Northern
T668XTV	Stagecoach EM	V909DDY	Stagecoach SE	X48CNY	Bebb Travel	Y808MFT	Go-Northern
T669XTV	Stagecoach EM	V943JST	Rapsons	X143WNL	Arriva North East	Y966PHL	Yorkshire Traction
T870RGA	Yorkshire Traction	V944JST	Rapsons	X144WNL	Arriva North East	Y967PHL	Yorkshire Traction
T871RGA	Yorkshire Traction	W30DTS	Durham Travel	X191HFB	First – Somerset	YJ51EKX	Selwyns
T872RGA	Yorkshire Traction	W226CDN	Selwyns	X192HFB	First – Somerset	YJ51EKY	Selwyns
TDZ3265	First - Avon	W381UEL	Bournemouth	X193HFB	First – Somerset	YJ51EKZ	Selwyns
TRM144	Rapsons	W382UEL	Bournemouth	X194HFB	First – Somerset	YN51XMH	Trathens
V10NAT	Bruce's	W383UEL	Bournemouth	X421WVO	Birmingham Coach	YN51XMJ	Trathens
V141EJR	Arriva North East	W384UEL	Bournemouth	X422WVO	Birmingham Coach	YN51XMK	Trathens
V142EJR	Arriva North East	W431RBB	Durham Travel	X423WVO	Birmingham Coach	YN51XML	Trathens
V209JAL	Trent	W432RBB	Durham Travel	X465XAS	Rapsons	YN51XMU	Trathens
V210JAL	Trent	W634MKY	Yeomans	X913ERA	Trent	YN51XMV	Trathens
V211JAL	Trent	W844SKH	East Yorkshire	X914ERA	Trent	YN51XMW	Trathens
V212JAL	Trent	WK02UMA	First – Devon & C	X915ERA	Trent	YN51XMX	Trathens
V215EGV	Galloway	WK02UMB	First – Devon & C	XSU612	Stagecoach SE	YN51XMZ	Trathens
V345EKW	Yorkshire Traction	WK02UMC	First – Devon & C	Y93HTX	Bebb Travel	YN51XNC	Trathens
V447EAL	Dunn-Line	WSV570	Arriva North East	Y94HTX	Bebb Travel	YN51XND	Trathens
V448EAL	Dunn-Line	WSV571	Arriva North East	Y96HTX	Bebb Travel	YN51XNE	Trathens
V449EAL	Dunn-Line	WSV572	Arriva North East	Y97HTX	Bebb Travel	YP02AAV	Birmingham Coach
V838JAT	East Yorkshire	WV02EUP	First - Avon	Y445XAT	East Yorkshire	YP02AAX	Birmingham Coach
V839JAT	East Yorkshire	WV02EUR	First - Avon	Y467HUA	Selwyns	YS02YXR	Yorkshire Traction
V840JAT	East Yorkshire	WV02EUT	First - Avon	Y468HUA	Selwyns	YS02YXT	Yorkshire Traction
V841JAT	East Yorkshire	WV02EUU	First - Avon	Y469HUA	Selwyns	YSU874	Go-Northern
V842JAT	East Yorkshire	WX51AJU	First – Somerset	Y475HUA	Selwyns	YSU875	Go-Northern
V843JAT	East Yorkshire	WX51AJV	First – Somerset	Y476HUA	Selwyns	YSU876	Go-Northern
V904DPN	Stagecoach SE	WX51AJY	First – Somerset	Y781MFT	Go-Northern	YTC838	Yorkshire Traction
V905DPN	Stagecoach SE	WX51AKY	First – Somerset	Y782MFT	Go-Northern	YX02JFY	East Yorkshire

ISBN 1 897990 58 8

© Published by *British Bus Publishing Ltd*, September 2002
British Bus Publishing Ltd, 16 St Margaret's Drive, Wellington, Telford, TF1 3PH
httm//www.britishbuspublishing.co.uk - Telephone: 01952 255669 - Facsimile: 01952 222397

The National Express Handbook